HELP ME GET READY TO READ

The Practical Guide For Reading Aloud
To Children During Their First Five Years

by Susan Marx and Barbara Kasok

Permissions
Reprinted with the permission of Simon & Schuster Books for Young Readers, an imprint of Simon & Schuster Children's Publishing Division from BLUE GOOSE by Nancy Tafuri. Copyright © 2008 Nancy Tafuri. Excerpts from SHEEP IN A JEEP by Nancy Shaw, illustrated by Margot Apple. Illustrations copyright ©1986 by Margot Apple. Reprinted by permission of Houghton Mifflin Harcourt Publishing Company. All rights reserved. Credit to Candlewick Press for use of HOORAY FOR FISH! by Lucy Cousins copyright © 2005 Lucy Cousins and ONE DUCK STUCK by Phyllis Root, illustrated by Jane Chapman copyright © 1998; Houghton Mifflin Harcourt Publishing Company for the use of PUFFINS CLIMB, PENGUINS RHYME by Bruce McMillan ©1995; Penguin Group for the use of THE SNOWY DAY by Ezra Jack Keats © 1962.

Contact us at: www.readaloudguide.com
Discounts available for bulk orders.

With love to my children—
Jenny and Alex, Amy and Rob, and Beth and Dan,
and to my grandchildren—
Noah, Abby, Johanna, Sophie, Jacob, Esther,
Madeline, and Ruby
                    SM

With love to my daughters—
Susan, Sharon, and Sarah,
and to my grandchildren—
Samantha and Jake
for sharing the joy of reading aloud with me
through the years.
                    BK

CONTENTS

Dear Reader,

In our "Help Me Get Ready To Read" workshops, we meet many parents and grandparents, early childhood educators, pre-school staff, daycare providers, librarians, and volunteers in literacy programs. This guide is written for such caring adults.

We often ask our workshop participants, "What do you like about reading aloud to little ones?" Some of you say that it is fun to read aloud—you love to laugh with children at silly pictures in books. Some tell us that reading aloud helps you bond with children—you love to sit with little ones close by. Still others respond that reading aloud helps children learn to enjoy books—you love to spend time together reading and rereading favorite books.

As mothers and grandmothers who have read books over the years to our own children and grandchildren, we agree with these responses. We know first-hand that reading aloud from infancy through the preschool years is a heartwarming experience for both adults and the young children in their lives.

As reading professionals and teachers, we also know that reading aloud during these formative years helps raise reading-ready children. Beginning in their earliest years, infants and toddlers make positive connections to books as they develop listening and speaking skills. Many 3-to-5 year olds continue to develop these and other early literacy concepts and skills as they listen to and talk about books. Reading aloud during the first five years of children's lives opens their ears to the sounds of words, their eyes to the wonder of pictures, their minds to new ideas, and their hearts to a love of books and learning.

While many adults realize the importance of reading aloud to young children, they do not always make the connection between reading aloud and getting children ready to read. They often ask us, "How can I help children get ready to read?" We respond by telling them they can do so by understanding early literacy concepts and skills, choosing good books to read aloud, and creating a nurturing environment in which little ones can thrive.

So we asked ourselves, "What can we do to help caring adults get children ready to learn to read?" There are many how-to books—why not one for adults that suggests ways to use both positive parenting strategies and reading strategies when reading aloud to children from infancy through the preschool years. The idea of providing such a guide appealed to our passion for helping children become lifelong readers and lovers of learning.

Thus, **Help Me Get Ready To Read** was born—an easy-to-follow guide offering parents and professionals practical strategies and activities to introduce children to early literacy concepts and skills. We use the word *parent* to include ALL adults who read aloud to young children. **Help Me Get Ready To Read** can be used when reading aloud to one or more children at home or when reading aloud to groups of children in daycare, preschool, or library settings.

The purpose of our guide is to help young children get ready to learn to read—<u>not</u> to teach them how to read. We hope **Help Me Get Ready To Read** reassures you that it is possible to have a positive impact on children's lives by reading aloud. You not only share good times together, but also foster a child's feelings of confidence and competence so that he or she will be ready to learn to read. Both you and the children in your lives reap countless benefits.

Happy Reading Aloud,
Susan Marx and Barbara Kasok

PART I

READING ALOUD TO INFANTS, TODDLERS, AND PRESCHOOLERS

1

UNDERSTANDING EARLY LITERACY CONCEPTS AND SKILLS

What would you do before starting off on a trip to a place you have not been to before? You might read a travel guide to learn about sites to visit, where to eat, and things to do. Perhaps, you might learn a few words or expressions if you don't already speak the language. Also, you might make a list of necessary things to take along. Such actions make you feel comfortable before you leave home. Your travel experiences will be more enjoyable, less stressful, and, most certainly, you will make better use of your time.

Just as a travel guide helps you prepare for a visit to a new place, *Help Me Get Ready To Read* is a guide that helps you prepare for the journey of getting children ready to learn to read. You can learn about early literacy concepts and skills and their importance based on current research. Also, you can become familiar with ways to introduce these concepts and skills while reading aloud.

According to the National Institute of Child Health and Human Development, early literacy is what children know about reading and writing before they actually learn to read and write. Young children can learn about reading and writing through the read-aloud experience. Making the read-aloud experience effective will foster feelings of comfort, competence, and confidence in children.

A favorite children's folktale "The Three Little Pigs" helps us understand the importance of early literacy concepts and skills.

As the story begins, the three little pigs are sent off into the world. Each little pig builds a house. The first little pig builds a house of straw. The second little pig builds a house of sticks. The third little pig builds a house of bricks. The houses made of straw and sticks fall apart easily. The house made of bricks does not. We learn a valuable lesson from the third little pig—strong building blocks create a sturdy framework.

Those of us who care about reading and young children can apply the lesson learned from the folktale to understand the significance of the early literacy concepts and skills. These early literacy concepts and skills are the strong building blocks children need to build a solid framework to be ready to learn to read.

Early Literacy Concepts and Skills

The importance of providing children with knowledge of early literacy concepts and skills before they enter school is confirmed in the comprehensive report "Developing Early Literacy" by the National Early Literacy Panel (NELP)(2008). Using data from 300 scientific studies on the development of early literacy skills in children from infancy to age five, NELP findings conclude that knowledge of early literacy skills leads to reading success, and most significantly, adults can help children develop these concepts and skills. What do such findings mean to you? Simply stated, reading aloud is a powerful tool to use to introduce early literacy concepts and skills to young children.

Early literacy concepts and skills include listening and speaking, vocabulary, comprehension, phonological awareness, print concepts, letters and their sounds, and writing. Let's look at each of these concepts and skills to find out how you can help children acquire them.

Listening and Speaking

If you want to help children develop listening and speaking skills,

Then ask them to listen for a purpose; respond to questions; tell about an experience or story; recite rhymes and poems; sing songs; describe people, places, and things; suggest ideas; and follow directions.

Vocabulary

If you want to help children develop vocabulary,

Then ask them to use picture clues and story events to understand new words; name people, places, and things; use action words; describe objects and events; and group words into categories, such as foods, shapes, colors, numbers, and time.

Comprehension

If you want to help children develop an understanding of text in different kinds of books, such as fiction and nonfiction,

Then encourage them to use pictures; talk about story characters, settings, and events; discuss a story problem and solution; make predictions about a story; relate their own experiences; retell a story; and tell if a story is make-believe or real.

Phonological Awareness

If you want to help children develop awareness of sounds that they hear in words,

Then ask them to listen to and recite rhymes; identify rhyming words; use rhyming words to complete sentences; rhyme one word with another; identify beginning and ending sounds in words; clap the words; and tap the word parts (syllables).

Print Concepts

If you want to help children develop an understanding of how print works,

Then show them how to hold a book and turn the pages, where to begin reading text on a page, and how print is read from left-to-right and top-to-bottom; point out that words are made up of letters, there are spaces between words, and sentences are made up of words; point out punctuation, such as question marks and periods; explain the words *title, author,* and *illustrator;* and identify types of everyday print, such as newspapers, signs, labels, and menus.

Letters and Their Sounds

If you want to help children develop an understanding of letters and their sounds,

Then ask them to recite the alphabet; name uppercase and lowercase letters; connect sounds with letters; recognize their names; and identify letters in their names.

Writing

If you want to help children develop an understanding that speech is print written down,

Then ask them to draw pictures and write about them; dictate words and sentences about their pictures; and form letters and write the letters in their names. Also, you can model how writing conveys meaning by pointing out street signs, labels, and menus.

Key Ideas about Early Literacy Concepts and Skills

There are two key ideas about these early literacy concepts and skills that are important to remember as you read aloud. These key ideas help you understand that early literacy concepts and skills are flexible rather than rigid regarding both a time frame and an order in which children acquire them.

Key Idea 1

Early literacy concepts and skills develop beginning in infancy.

We recommend that you start to read aloud early in a child's first year. You can read nursery rhymes and sing lullabies to newborns as you cuddle them in your arms. Listening to words introduces your littlest ones to the sounds of language. Hearing your calming voice and feeling your warmth is soothing and comforting to an infant. Infants, as with all children, thrive when you give them your focused attention.

When reading aloud during a child's first two years, we suggest that you do the following: point to the pictures in the book; respond to your little one's attention span rather than focusing on finishing the book; encourage interaction by having your little ones help turn the pages, hold the book, lift the flaps on the pages, point to the pictures and join in saying words and phrases; and reread the same books over time so they become familiar to your little ones.

As infants and toddlers grow and develop into preschoolers, they continue to build their knowledge of early literacy concepts and skills as they listen to and talk about what happens in stories and notice how print works.

Key Idea 2

Early literacy concepts and skills are acquired over time in different ways.

As you read aloud the same book over a span of five years, children develop early literacy concepts and skills. You can introduce these concepts and skills one at a time during different readings. For example, when reading a book you can focus on vocabulary during one read-aloud time, and comprehension during another reading of the same book. Or, you can introduce more than one early literacy concept and skill when reading aloud since many of them overlap. Such an example might be introducing both vocabulary and comprehension during the same reading.

2

CHOOSING GOOD BOOKS TO READ ALOUD

Have you ever spent time standing in the children's room of your community library or in a bookstore wondering which book to pull off the shelf? It can be overwhelming to see shelves loaded with books and difficult to know which books are best suited to your child.

Parents often ask us, "What are good books to read to my child?" We respond by telling them that good books entertain, encourage discussion, spark imagination, and provide information. When you choose good books, you provide fun-filled reading experiences that are also learning opportunities.

The criteria that follow can help you choose appropriate books for children while browsing in neighborhood libraries, bookstores, and online. We suggest that you try to select a variety of children's books that:

- introduce sounds of language with repetitive, rhyming, or predictable text;
- use engaging illustrations along with text;
- contain content that relates to your child's experiences and interests;
- go beyond your child's life experiences;
- provide stories with problems and solutions;
- reflect diversity in story characters, authors, and illustrators;
- include a range of genres, such as fiction, nonfiction, folktales, rhymes, and songs; and
- represent well-known authors and illustrators as well as new authors and illustrators.

You might wonder where to find books that you can read aloud to young children that meet these criteria. Librarians in your community along with parents, early childhood professionals in preschools, staff at daycare centers, and children's literature websites are some resources you can use to learn about quality books. Based on our experiences over the years reading aloud to many different groups of young children, we have our own favorites to recommend. Some are classics that may be familiar to you. Others are new books by contemporary authors and illustrators. The books cover a range of topics that are popular with young children.

We arranged these recommended books into two age groups to make it easy for you to select appropriate books for children. The books for infants and toddlers are suitable for little ones from birth to 2 years old. The books for 3-to-5 year olds are more appropriate for preschoolers because of their content and format.

You might consider looking at both lists when choosing books because there is no real distinction between them. For example, many toddlers enjoy listening to books about story characters while many 3-to-5 year olds delight in hearing simpler books that have been read to them since infancy. So try to keep in mind a child's age and stage of development when choosing good books to read aloud. Also, remember that introducing children to a variety of texts, such as fiction and nonfiction, helps them become lifelong lovers of reading and learning.

Our Recommended Books for Infants and Toddlers

As we mentioned previously, from birth to 2 years of age, little ones develop early literacy concepts and skills as you read aloud and talk about books. These little ones acquire language by listening to you and, in time, using the words they hear to speak on their own. When you read aloud these recommended books, infants and toddlers enjoy listening to the sounds of language and looking at the pictures. In addition, the rhyming, repetitive, and patterned text, along with the colorful illustrations, introduces them to the exciting world of books. Here are some of our favorite books to read aloud to this age group.

All the World by Liz Garton Scanlon, illustrated by Marla Frazee, Beach Lane, 2009. Engaging illustrations and simple text show how our beautiful world belongs to all of us.

Baby Animals by Gyo Fujikawa, Sterling, 2008. The sounds baby animals make, how they feel, and what they do are described in this book with illustrations that appeal to young children.

Big Fat Hen by Keith Baker, Harcourt, 1994. Based on the counting rhyme "One, Two, Buckle My Shoe," there are lots of things to count in a barnyard filled with chickens and hens.

Black on White by Tana Hoban, Greenwillow, 1993. This wordless book uses photographs of objects and animals to capture children's interest.

Blue Hat, Green Hat by Sandra Boynton, Little Simon, 1984. Silly cartoon animals introduce color words in this popular Boynton book.

The Bridge is Up! by Babs Bell, illustrated by Rob Heffernan, Harper, 2004. Different vehicles that children often see in their everyday lives have to wait in line on the road because the bridge is up.

Clap Your Hands by Lorinda Bryan Cauley, Putnam, 1997. Children and animals have a good time as they clap, dance, jump, and spin through the day.

Dancing Feet by Lindsey Craig, illustrated by Marc Brown, Knopf, 2010. Children are asked to guess what animal is dancing in this book with rhyming, repetitive text.

Each Peach Pear Plum by Janet and Alan Ahlberg, Viking, 1999. Rhyming text invites young children to discover nursery rhyme characters in the illustrations.

Good Night, Gorilla by Peggy Rathmann, Putnam, 2003. Detailed illustrations tell a funny story about zoo animals that follow a zookeeper home one night.

Hello, Day! by Anita Lobel, Greenwillow, 2008. Repetitive text tells about the sounds animals make.

Here a Chick, Where a Chick? by Suse MacDonald, Scholastic, 2004. Different farm animals can be found hidden under the flaps on the pages in this interactive book.

Here Are My Hands by Bill Martin Jr and John Archambault, illustrated by Ted Rand, Holt, 1985. Rhyming text describes different body parts and how they are used.

Hooray for Fish! by Lucy Cousins, Candlewick, 2005. Appealing illustrations and text hold children's interest in this story about a little fish that swims around meeting other fish while it looks for its mother.

Hop Jump by Ellen Stoll Walsh, Harcourt, 1993. In this amusing story, frogs learn to dance when they become bored with hopping and jumping.

I Went Walking by Sue Williams, illustrated by Julie Vivas, Harcourt, 1990. A young child sees animals of different colors while taking a walk.

The Little School Bus by Carol Roth, illustrated by Pamela Papparone, North-South, 2002. A variety of humorous animals ride the bus to and from school in this book with repetitive and predictable text.

Moo Moo, Brown Cow by Jakki Wood, illustrated by Rog Bonner, Harcourt, 1992. The repetitive text tells about a kitten that asks farm animals about their babies.

My Baby & Me by Lynn Reiser, photographs by Penny Genticu, Knopf, 2008. Engaging text and photographs show babies and toddlers of varied ethnicities doing many activities.

One Duck Stuck by Phyllis Root, illustrated by Jane Chapman, Candlewick, 1998. Different animals try to free one duck that gets stuck in the muck in this counting book.

One Pup's Up by Marsha Wilson Chall, illustrated by Henry Cole, McElderry Books, 2010. The rhyming text and fun illustrations in this counting story about ten puppies capture young children's attention.

Peek-a-Who? by Nina Laden, Chronicle, 2000. In this book with simple rhyming text, children guess who is looking through the peek-a-who windows.

Sheep in a Jeep by Nancy Shaw, illustrated by Margot Apple, Houghton, 1988. Rhyming words tell this story about five sheep that go on a hilarious adventure.

Sometimes I Like to Curl Up in a Ball by Vicki Churchill, illustrated by Charles Fuge, Sterling, 2001. Appealing illustrations and rhyming text tell a story about a cute little wombat.

Spot Can Count by Eric Hill, Putnam, 1999. Spot counts the farm animals in this interactive book.

The Three Bears by Byron Barton, Harper, 1991. This popular folktale is about Mama, Papa, and Baby Bear and their unexpected encounter with Goldilocks.

Time for Bed by Mem Fox, illustrated by Jane Dyer, Gulliver, 1993. Illustrations of baby animals bedding down for the night and rhyming couplets make this a good bedtime read aloud.

Toes, Ears, & Nose! by Marion Dane Bauer, illustrated by Karen Katz, Little Simon, 2003. In this interactive book, children lift the flaps on the pages to discover body parts.

Where Does Maisy Live? by Lucy Cousins, Walker, 2000. Children find out where Maisy lives by lifting the flaps on the pages in this interactive book.

Where Is Tippy Toes? by Betsy Lewin, Atheneum, 2010. Rhyming text and engaging illustrations tell the story of a cat named Tippy Toes that goes places during the day and arrives at a special place at night.

Where to Sleep by Kandy Radzinski, Sleeping Bear, 2009. Rhyming text tells how a kitten looks for different places to sleep.

Whose Chick Are You? by Nancy Tafuri, Greenwillow, 2007. Animals try to answer the question in the book title.

Our Recommended Books for 3-to-5 Year Olds

We encourage you to read the books recommended for infants and toddlers to 3-to-5 year olds as well. Preschoolers enjoy these same books whether they have listened to them before, or are hearing them for the first time.

In addition, we provide a list of recommended books specifically for children in this age group because they are ready for books that are more complex in both language and content. You can read aloud these books to 3-to-5 year olds to help them acquire early literacy concepts and skills, such as identifying story characters, settings, events, and understanding problems and solutions.

At the Beach by Anne and Harlow Rockwell, Simon & Schuster, 1987. A young girl and her mother discover sandpipers, seaweed, seashells, and little fish while spending a day at the beach.

Baby Can by Eve Bunting, illustrated by Maxie Chambliss, Boyds Mills, 2007. A big brother shows what he can do after the arrival of a new baby in the family.

Bear Snores On by Karma Wilson, illustrated by Jane Chapman, McElderry, 2001. Bear wakes up from a long winter's sleep in his cave too late to be a part of his friends' party.

Blue Goose by Nancy Tafuri, Simon & Schuster, 2008. Blue Goose, Red Hen, Yellow Chick, and White Duck decide to paint Farmer Gray's farm while he is away.

Bumpety Bump! by Pat Hutchins, Greenwillow, 2006. A young boy shows all he can do on his grandfather's farm.

Bunny Bungalow by Cynthia Rylant, illustrated by Nancy Hayashai, Harcourt, 1999. A bunny family makes their new bungalow into a cozy home.

Chicken Bedtime Is Really Early by Erica S. Perl, illustrated by George Bates, Abrams, 2005. All through the night, different animal mothers and fathers get their little ones to sleep.

Firehouse by Mark Teague, Orchard, 2010. In this amusing book, two dogs learn how things work during a visit to a firehouse.

Five Little Monkeys With Nothing To Do by Eileen Christelow, Clarion, 1996. Five monkeys clean the house before Grandma's visit, but mess it up again after picking berries.

Hattie and the Fox by Mem Fox, illustrated by Patricia Mullins, Macmillan, 1986. When Hattie tries to warn the other barnyard animals about a fox hiding in the bushes, no one pays attention.

Hey Mr. Choo-choo, Where Are You Going? by Susan Wickberg, illustrated by Yumi Heo, Putnam, 2008. The rhyming and repetitive text tells about places that a train visits.

Hickory Dickory Dock by Keith Baker, Harcourt, 2007. A mouse and other animals run up and down a clock in this adaptation of a favorite children's nursery rhyme.

Is Your Mama a Llama? by Deborah Guerney, illustrated by Steve Kellogg, Scholastic, 1989. A baby llama named Lloyd asks different animal friends if their mama is a llama.

Jesse Bear, What Will You Wear? by Nancy White Carlstrom, illustrated by Bruce Degen, Simon & Schuster, 1986. Jesse Bear wears different things from morning until night.

Kitty Cat, Kitty Cat, Are You Waking Up? by Bill Martin Jr and Michael Sampson, illustrated by Laura J. Bryant, Marshall Cavendish, 2008. Kitty Cat has a hard time getting ready for school.

Like a Windy Day by Frank Asch and Devin Asch, Gulliver, 2002. A young girl likes to do all the things that the wind does.

The Little Rabbit Who Liked to Say MOO by Jonathan Allen, Boxer, 2008. The use of text bubbles helps tell the story of animals who decide to say the sounds that other animals make.

The Little Red Hen by Byron Barton, Harper, 1993. None of Red Hen's friends help her make bread, but they want to help her eat it.

Mama Cat Has Three Kittens by Denise Fleming, Holt, 1998. Boris awakens from his nap just as Mama Cat's other kittens take their nap after doing lots of things.

Maybe a Bear Ate It! by Robie H. Harris, illustrated by Michael Emberley, Orchard, 2008. A silly critter looks all over imagining what might have happened to a lost book.

Millie Wants to Play! by Janet Pedersen, Candlewick, 2004. Millie is the first farm animal up in the morning eager to play.

Monkey Monkey Monkey by Cathy MacLennan, Boxer, 2009. Monkey explores the rainforest looking for monkey nuts only to discover that his mom and dad have lots of monkey nuts for him.

My Garden by Kevin Henkes, Greenwillow, 2010. In this entertaining story, a young girl pretends to plant all sorts of interesting things in her garden.

Pretend You're a Cat by Jean Marzollo, illustrated by Jerry Pinkney, Dial, 1990. Children respond to questions by imitating the sounds and actions of different animals.

Puffins Climb, Penguins Rhyme by Bruce McMillan, Gulliver, 1995. In this nonfiction book, photographs and rhyming text help children learn about puffins and penguins.

Silly Tilly by Eileen Spinelli, illustrated by David Slonim, Marshall Cavendish, 2009. Silly Tilly's friends get tired of her being silly all the time, but later miss the fun when she stops making them laugh.

The Snowy Day by Ezra Jack Keats, Viking, 1962. In this classic story, a boy named Peter wakes up on a wintry morning eager to play outside.

Subway by Anastasia Suen, illustrated by Karen Katz, Viking, 2004. Rhythmic text and colorful illustrations make a subway ride come alive.

Together by Jane Simmons, Knopf, 2007. Mousse and Nut are two dogs that find out what it means to be a real friend.

Turtle Splash! by Cathryn Falwell, Greenwillow, 2001. In this counting book, turtles splash into the water as other pond creatures disturb their peaceful day.

Turtle's Penguin Day by Valeri Gorbachev, Knopf, 2008. Turtle pretends to be a penguin after hearing a bedtime story.

Warthogs Paint by Pamela Duncan Edwards, illustrated by Henry Cole, Hyperion, 2001. Warthogs learn about mixing colors as they paint their kitchen wall.

The Appendix has more recommended books for infants and toddlers on pages 131-135 and for 3-to-5 year olds on pages 135-141.

Also, there is a list of suggested alphabet books on pages 141-142. These books are appropriate for you to read to both age groups. Reading aloud alphabet books is a fun way to help introduce little ones to letters of the alphabet.

Our recommended rhyme, fingerplay, and song books on pages 143-144 provide opportunities for you to add movement and music to the read-aloud experience. These books are suitable for children starting in infancy through the preschool years.

3

CREATING A LOVE OF BOOKS AND LEARNING

After a busy day, many infants, toddlers, and preschoolers look forward to listening to a bedtime story as part of their nightly routine. Why is reading aloud something they enjoy? They like the comforting feeling of being with you after a hectic day filled with lots of activities. Reading aloud at bedtime, and at any other time during the day, is quality parenting at its best—a time when both you and your child feel an emotional connection—a time when both you and your child feel good about being together. Whenever you read aloud, you convey a loving message to children.

I want to read this book to you because I care about
you, I respect you, and I value our time together.

The read-aloud experience is a meaningful way for you to engage in effective parenting by modeling positive discipline, encouraging healthy communication, and fostering good self-esteem. The time you spend reading aloud supports children's emotional, social, language, and cognitive development. It is important to remember that children develop according to their own timeline. Also, keep in mind that each child is unique with his or her own temperament and personality as well as likes and dislikes. During the read-aloud experience, children grow because they learn, create, imagine, and play.

Furthermore, creating a cozy, loving environment helps children bond both with you and books. A child receives your focused attention, feels comfortable about learning, and has opportunities to show off new things he or she can do. Here are positive parenting suggestions that make the read-aloud time a worthwhile experience.

Create a nurturing environment to foster children's self-esteem and encourage communication.

- Keep in mind each child's age and stage of development, interests, and attention span.
- Give each child positive feedback.
- Find a quiet place to read.
- Turn off the TV.
- Try to not answer the phone.
- Point out connections between story events and what happens in real life.
- Talk with children about the story.
- Connect books you read together by pointing out similarities between them.

Establish reading routines so that books and learning become a part of children's everyday lives.

- Set up regular reading times, such as naptime, bedtime, or regular story times during the day or week.
- Place books in a basket or on a shelf so they are accessible to children.
- Encourage children to select books that they want to hear.
- Avoid reading scary books at bedtime.
- Take favorite books on vacation with you.
- Arrange library visits as a regular activity.
- Swap books with other families.

Model having a positive attitude towards books and learning.

- Read aloud books that convey healthy values.
- Tell children how much you enjoy reading books together.

- Give books as gifts.
- Laugh when reading silly books with children.
- Read in your own free time.
- Handle books with care.
- Use library resources and book reviews to find out about new children's books.

Questions Parents Often Ask

In our workshops, we are asked questions about reading aloud to children during their first five years. Many of the questions are common concerns expressed by parents and other caring adults. Here is a sampling of some questions and responses.

1. What kinds of books would be good to read to my baby?

There are many books available that are appropriate for your littlest ones. Try to select books with simple repetitive text—words or phrases that are repeated over and over again. Also, look for books with such features as rhyming words, black and white illustrations or photographs, and large colorful illustrations. Board books are especially suitable for this age group because of their durability. There are recommended read-aloud books for infants and toddlers in Chapter 2 and in the Appendix.

2. Is it okay to read the same book over and over again?

We encourage parents to reread books to their young children. As children become familiar with a book, it becomes one they like because they can join in with words and phrases, and know what happens in the story. How excited children feel when they listen to a book in kindergarten that is an old favorite. Can't you hear a child saying—*I know that book!*

3. What do I do if a child gets restless while I'm reading aloud?

Read-aloud times should be stress-free so be sure to have realistic expectations for children. If a child needs to move around or has a short attention span, adjust your reading and reading time. For example, if a child seems to be loosing interest in the book as you read aloud, stop reading and tell the child that you will finish reading the book at another time.

Or, instead of reading the book, you may do a picture walk using the pictures to tell what happens in your own words. This strategy takes less time and gives the child a sense of accomplishment. Be sure to take the time to acknowledge the good job your child is doing sitting with you, listening to the story, and looking at the pictures.

In Chapter 5, "Applying Early Literacy Concepts and Skills to Six Favorite Children's Books," you will find **Positive Parenting Praise!** models that show how to give positive feedback to children as they get ready to learn to read.

4. What do I do when a child wants to read books only on one topic, such as dinosaurs?

Don't discourage a child's interest in a topic that you know is a good one. For many little ones, dinosaurs are fun, scary, interesting, and spark imaginations. Go to your local library to find more dinosaur books , but also find a book or two on related topics, such as rainforest animals or farm animals.

5. How do I respond when a child seems reluctant to take an active part in the read-aloud experience?

Responding to questions that you ask or engaging in discussions while reading aloud involves risk taking on the part of young children. Be sure to set realistic expectations by keeping in mind what each child is capable of doing. Some children are hesitant to take an active role because they are afraid of making a mistake and disappointing themselves as well as you. Remember to tell children to try their best. In that way, you are giving a child permission to try without creating the pressure to be perfect. Also, provide positive reinforcement while reading together to build children's confidence in learning new things.

6. What should I do when a child wants to try to read rather than listen to the book?

Many 3-to-4 year olds love to have an audience to show off what they can do. They like to pretend that they are reading, so definitely encourage children to do so. A child might read the book by telling the story in his or her own words, talking about the pictures in the book, recognizing and reading some words or reciting repetitive words or phrases.

Be sure to give **Positive Parenting Praise!** such as *Good job reading the book using your own words.* Positive feedback goes a long way in motivating children to learn to read. Also, it is worth noting that after children learn to read, they still benefit from being with you and enjoy listening as you read aloud to them.

7. What should I do when children do not show an interest in books?

In our age of technology, many parents find that television, video games, and electronic gadgets compete with books for children's attention. One suggestion is to encourage children to select their own books rather than choosing ones that you think will be of interest to them. You might talk with children about topics they like and find related books to read. Children's librarians can help you find appropriate books.

Another suggestion is to list titles of books that you read together on a reading chart. Encourage children to place stickers next to the book titles after you read them. This provides children with something tangible that can be a source of pride for them. Be sure to display their reading chart in a place where children can see them.

8. How can I make reading a family activity?

Some families schedule a nightly quiet time during which family members spend time looking at and reading printed materials, such as newspapers, books, magazines, and catalogues. In addition, some families plan regular outings to local libraries and bookstores to get books and attend children's story hour together.

9. How do I read to a 3-year-old and 5-year-old at the same time?

Before you begin reading aloud, tell children that sharing a book is a fun way to be together. Make sure both children are comfortable and can see the pages. Promote good listening and speaking skills by reminding children not to interrupt when someone else is speaking. Try to direct questions to each child at his or her level of understanding. In that way, children benefit from individual attention. As you read aloud, pause to give children **Positive Parenting Praise!**, such as telling them what a good job they are doing listening to the story.

10. How do I respond when my 6-year-old feels badly because a younger sibling is already reading?

Acknowledge the feelings of a 6-year-old by explaining that sometimes things that happen make us sad. Let your child know that everyone is different. Each of us learns to do things, such as walk, talk, ride a bike, and read when we are ready. When reading aloud together, be sure to take the time to point out things your child already knows how to do, such as recognizing letter names and sounds, identifying rhyming words, using picture clues, and telling how the story might end. Acknowledging what children can do boosts their self-esteem.

PART II

HELPING PRESCHOOLERS ACQUIRE EARLY LITERACY CONCEPTS AND SKILLS

4

USING *TALKABOUTS* AND *FOLLOW-UP FUN* WITH 3-TO-5 YEAR OLDS

In your everyday lives, you are juggling a lot of balls in the air, such as family responsibilities, work obligations, and the ever-increasing pressures of raising children in our world today. Yet, with your limited time, you want to do what is best for the children in your care.

Many adults who read to young children understand the importance of reading aloud but are not familiar with how to introduce early literacy concepts and skills to 3-to-5 year olds during the read-aloud experience. So, based on our experience as reading professionals and teachers, we created *Talkabout* book plans and *Follow-Up Fun* activities for you to use to help young children acquire early literacy concepts and skills by applying them to six recommended books.

Talkabouts

The *Talkabout* is a book plan that provides reading strategies you can implement when reading aloud to young children. There are five *Talkabouts* that focus on specific early literacy concepts and skills as follows:

- **Vocabulary** offers suggestions on how to introduce children to new words and their meanings.

- **Comprehension** provides prompts to use to encourage conversations that help children understand a story.
- **Phonological Awareness** suggests ways to help children listen for the sounds in words.
- **Print Concepts** models strategies you can use to help children understand how print works.
- **Letters and Their Sounds** shows how to help children recognize letters of the alphabet and connect sounds to letters.

Each *Talkabout* has three parts that are easy to follow. They are:

1. **Before you read** - models how to introduce the book by talking about the title, author, illustrator, or picture on the cover.
2. **As you read aloud** - provides reading strategies to use that help children develop early literacy concepts and skills.
3. **Finish reading** - suggests ideas for talking about how the story ends, story characters, or words used in the story.

In addition, within each *Talkabout,* there is an example of **Positive Parenting Praise!** It is a model that shows how you can give positive feedback to foster a child's social, emotional, and cognitive development during the read-aloud experience. **Positive Parenting Praise!** is a way to recognize a skill that a child acquires, such as turning the page, pointing to a letter, or reciting a rhyme along with you. It is also a way to recognize the effort a child makes as he or she takes the risk of learning a new skill.

Too often, parents with good intentions give a generic compliment, such as *I like your pretty picture* instead of specific praise for what a child actually does. An example of specific praise is *I like the bright colors in your picture.* The more specific your praise, the more meaningful it is to the child. Giving a child specific praise is important for several reasons. First, such positive feedback lets a child know that what he or she is doing is worthy of your praise. Secondly, it gives a child the message that you care because you are taking the time to notice details.

Take the time to acknowledge the little steps a child takes in getting ready to learn to read. It helps children make a positive connection to books and learning and gives them a good feeling about themselves. Be careful not to go overboard with your praise because when done too much, it loses its impact on children of any age. Rather, we recommend that you give **Positive Parenting Praise!** during read-aloud time when a child's accomplishments and efforts are deserving of it.

Follow-Up Fun

Follow-Up Fun consists of book-related activities to use to help children further develop early literacy concepts and skills while having a good time. You can do these activities after reading aloud with your child, or a group of children. The activities address the different interests and learning styles of young children by engaging them in movement, inviting them to join in rhymes and songs, involving them in creative projects, and having them listen to more read-aloud books.

The *Follow-Up Fun* activities are:

• Act & Play

In these dramatic play activities, children pretend to do things, such as play outside on a snowy day or be an animal. Such activities are often springboards that spark children's imaginations so that they add their own ideas to the read-aloud fun. While acting and playing, children are building their listening, speaking, and vocabulary skills.

• Say & Sing

Children develop listening and speaking skills along with phonological awareness skills when you introduce them to well-known rhymes, fingerplays, and songs, such as "Teddy Bear, Teddy Bear" and "The Wheels on the Bus." Young children enjoy listening to simple rhymes, tapping the word parts, and singing lively songs as they begin to join in with words and phrases, do simple finger motions, supply missing rhyming words or finish a line of a rhyme or poem.

- **Draw & Write**

These activities support children in becoming aware of print by taking part in activities, such as drawing pictures, making birthday cards, and creating mobiles. Also, children learn to recognize letters and their sounds as they watch you write and name letters or try to do so on their own.

Remember that as young children explore drawing and writing, you will notice a variety of responses. Some little ones need to be shown how to hold a crayon or pencil. Others might draw scribbles on the page while others draw pictures and begin to form letters. Be sure to give **Positive Parenting Praise!** that focuses on a specific task a child does, such as *Good job holding your crayon*, or *I like the brown horse that you drew in your farm picture.*

- **Read Aloud & Enjoy**

The books listed in this activity are related to the six favorite children's books by author, illustrator, or topic. As you read aloud books from these lists, be sure to use strategies in the *Talkabouts* to help children continue to develop early literacy concepts and skills. You might recite a rhyme, sing a song, or draw a picture as a *Follow-Up Fun* activity for these additional books. Remember that read-aloud time provides lots of creative opportunities.

Applying *Talkabouts* and *Follow-Up Fun*

In Chapter 5, we show you how to apply *Talkabouts* and *Follow-Up Fun* to six favorite children's books. The featured books are *Blue Goose* by Nancy Tafuri, *Hooray for Fish!* by Lucy Cousins, *One Duck Stuck* by Phyllis Root, *Puffins Climb, Penguins Rhyme* by Bruce McMillan, *Sheep in a Jeep* by Nancy Shaw, and *The Snowy Day* by Ezra Jack Keats. These books are readily available in libraries, bookstores, and online.

Of course, you are not limited to these books, but they are a good collection of books to use when you begin to introduce early literacy concepts and skills. We suggest that you get these books for your child, if possible, to start to a little library. After becoming familiar with the strategies in the *Talkabouts* for these books, you can apply the strategies to any book when reading aloud to young children.

When helping young children acquire early literacy concepts and skills try to maintain a comfortable environment that focuses on the fun of reading and being together. Remember reading strategies are not intended for use every time you read aloud. Look for "teachable moments" to help your child get ready to read. They are times when the text and illustrations lend themselves to engaging children in books.

In conclusion, encourage children's enthusiasm, listen to their ideas, and respond in positive ways. By doing so, reading aloud can become a favorite activity for both adults and children. Keeping the fun in reading aloud helps you raise reading-ready children who love books and learning.

5

APPLYING EARLY LITERACY CONCEPTS AND SKILLS TO SIX FAVORITE CHILDREN'S BOOKS

Use the **Talkabout** book plans and **Follow-Up Fun** activities for the six favorite children's books in this chapter to help 3-to-5 year olds acquire early literacy concepts and skills. You can get these featured books listed below at your library, at a local bookstore, or online.

Blue Goose
by Nancy Tafuri

Here are five *Talkabouts* to use when reading aloud *Blue Goose* to 3-to-5 year olds. Along with the *Talkabouts* are *Follow-Up Fun* activities to do after reading the book.

We suggest following the steps below to help children in this age group develop early literacy concepts and skills as you enjoy the read-aloud experience together.

Step 1 Read *Blue Goose* and the five *Talkabouts* on your own.

Step 2 Select the early literacy concepts and skills that you want to focus on as you read aloud to children.

Step 3 Read aloud *Blue Goose* using appropriate strategies for those concepts and skills.

Step 4 Reread *Blue Goose* at other times using different suggestions in the *Talkabouts.*

Step 5 Choose *Follow-Up Fun* activities to do after reading the book.

Talkabout

Blue Goose

Vocabulary

Before you read the story talk about the cover. You might say:

- The title of this book is **_Blue Goose._** Let's read the title together—**_Blue Goose._** Look at the farm animals on the cover. What farm animal says *Honk, honk? Quack, quack? Cluck, cluck? Peep, peep?* Let's read **_Blue Goose_** to listen for words that tell about the barnyard.

As you read aloud pause on the first page to name things in the barnyard. You might ask:

- What is the big building in the picture? Show me the barn.
- The shutters are closed on the barn windows. Show me the shutters.
- Can you point to the barn door?
- Is the roof on the top or bottom of the barn? Show me the roof.
- Show me the fence. Why is there a fence?
- Show me the tractor. Why does a farmer use a tractor?

Positive Parenting Praise! Good job pointing to things in the barnyard.

Finish reading the story pausing at the end to ask children to name and point to red, blue, yellow, white, and green things in the barnyard.

Talkabout

Blue Goose

Comprehension

Before you read the story talk about the cover. You might say:

- The title of this book is **Blue Goose**. Let's read the title together—**Blue Goose**. What animals do you see on the cover? Show me Blue Goose, White Duck, Red Hen, and Yellow Chick. Let's read the story to find out what the animals paint.

As you read aloud talk about the story problem and what the animals do to solve it. You might ask:

- Why are the animals waving to Farmer Gray? Let's say together—*Good-bye Farmer Gray!*
- Let's look at the barnyard at the beginning of the story. Do you see lots of colors? Do the animals like the way the barnyard looks?
- What do you see in the wheel barrow? What will the animals do while Farmer Gray is away?
- Can animals really paint a barnyard?
- How does Blue Goose get on the roof? Let's say together—*Watch out Blue Goose, don't fall!*

Positive Parenting Praise! Good job telling Blue Goose to be careful.

- How does the barnyard look when Farmer Gray comes back?

Finish reading the story pausing to ask children if Farmer Gray likes the way the barnyard looks after the animals paint it.

Talkabout
Blue Goose

Phonological Awareness

Before you read the story talk about the beginning and ending sounds in the word *Goose* in the title. You might say:

- The title of this story is **Blue Goose.** Listen as I say the word *Goose*. What sound do you hear first in *Goose?* Listen as I say the word *Goose* again. What sound do you hear last in *Goose?*

As you read aloud pause on the first few pages to identify beginning and ending sounds in words. You might say:

- Listen as I say the word *duck*. What sound do you hear first in *duck?*
- Listen again to the word *duck*. What sound do you hear last in *duck?*

Positive Parenting Praise! Good job listening for beginning and ending sounds in *duck*.

- Listen as I say the word *hen*. What sound do you hear first in *hen?* What sound do you hear last in *hen?*

Finish reading the story pausing to have children tell the first and last sounds they hear in the word *pig*.

Talkabout
Blue Goose

Print Concepts

Before you read the story talk about the title. You might say:

- The title of this book is ***Blue Goose***. Watch as I move my finger under the words in the title as I read them aloud. Say the words with me—***Blue Goose.*** I'll point to the space between the two words. Show me the space between the two words.

Positive Parenting Praise! Good job pointing to the space between words.

As you read aloud pause to point out how print is read from left-to-right. You might say:

- Watch my finger as I move it under the words that I read on this page.
- Show me where to begin reading the words on the page.
- Show me where to stop reading the words on the page.
- I'll point to a space between two words.
- Show me the space between two words.

Finish reading the story pausing to move your finger under the letters in the word *Surprise!* Have children name the letters and shout with you—*Surprise!*

Talkabout
Blue Goose

Letters and Their Sounds

Before you read the story talk about uppercase letter *G* in the title. You might say:

- The title of this book is ***Blue Goose***. Listen as I say the word *Goose*. What sound do you hear first in *Goose*? Say the sound with me—/g/ /g/ /g/.* Uppercase letter *G* stands for the /g/ sound. Point to uppercase letter *G* with me.

As you read aloud pause to point to uppercase letter *G* in *Goose*. You might say:

- What sound do you hear first in *Goose*? Say the sound with me—/g/ /g/ /g/.
- Uppercase letter *G* stands for the /g/ sound.
- Point to uppercase letter *G* with me.

Positive Parenting Praise! Good job saying the /g/ sound and pointing to uppercase letter *G*.

Finish reading the story having children say /g//g//g/ when they hear the word *Goose*.

Letter Chant Children can giggle as they chant *G* is for *Goose* /g/ /g/ /g/.

*The symbol // is used to show the sound a letter stands for. For example, the sound at the beginning of the word *Goose* is the /g/ sound.

Follow-Up Fun
Blue Goose

Act & Play

Let's pretend to be animals in the story.

Let's be White Duck.
Waddle like a duck to the fence.
Paint the fence white. Dip the brush—*Dip, dip, dip!*
Let's say—*Quack, quack, quack!*

Let's be Yellow Chick.
Hop like a chick to the flowers.
Paint the flowers yellow. Bend down low—*Swish, swish, swish!*
Let's say—*Peep, peep, peep!*
Positive Parenting Praise! Good job painting the flowers.

Let's be Red Hen.
Run like a hen to the barn.
Paint the barn red. Reach way up—*High, high, high!*
Let's say—*Cluck, cluck, cluck!*

Let's be Blue Goose.
Fly like a goose to the roof.
Paint the roof blue. Take a bow—*Clap, clap, clap!*
Let's say—*Honk, honk, honk!*

Follow-Up Fun
Blue Goose

Say & Sing

Old Farmer Gray Had a Farm

Old Farmer Gray had a farm,　(7 taps)
E-i-e-i-o!　(5 taps)
And on that farm he had a goose,　(8 taps)
E-i-e-i-o!　(5 taps)
With a *honk, honk* here,　(5 taps)
And a *honk, honk* there.　(5 taps)
Here a *honk,* there a *honk,*　(6 taps)
Everywhere a *honk, honk.*　(5 taps)
Old Farmer Gray had a farm,　(7 taps)
E-i-e-i-o!　(5 taps)

What to Say

- Listen as I sing the song about a farm.
- Let's sing the song and tap the word parts together.

Positive Parenting Praise! Good job singing and tapping the word parts.

- Let's sing the song naming other farm animals and the sounds they make, such as a chick—*peep, peep;* a duck—*quack, quack;* a hen—*cluck, cluck;* and a horse—*neigh, neigh.*

Follow-Up Fun
Blue Goose

Draw & Write

Let's draw a barnyard.

What You Need
drawing paper, crayons or markers

What to Do

1. Have children draw a picture of a barnyard.
Positive Parenting Praise! Good job using colors in your barnyard picture.
2. Ask children to tell about their pictures. Record their responses on their pictures. If children want to write on their own using scribbles or letters, encourage them to do so.
3. Write children's names on their pictures using uppercase letters. Name each letter as you write.
4. Display the barnyard pictures.

Follow-Up Fun
Blue Goose

Read Aloud & Enjoy

If your child enjoys **Blue Goose** by Nancy Tafuri, we suggest the following book by the same author:

Have You Seen My Duckling? by Nancy Tafuri, Greenwillow, 1984. Mother Duck goes around the pond asking if any of the animals have seen her missing duckling.

Here are more books about farm animals and colors.

Big Red Barn by Margaret Wise Brown, illustrated by Felicia Bond, Harper, 1989. A variety of big and small animals spend a busy day on a farm.

Hurry! Hurry! by Eve Bunting, illustrated by Jeff Mack, Harcourt, 2007. In the story's surprise ending, all the animals rush to see a chick hatching.

Mouse Paint by Ellen Stoll Walsh, Harcourt, 1989. Three white mice mix colors in three paint jars—red, blue, and yellow.

WOW! Said the Owl by Tim Hopgood, Farrar, Straus and Giroux, 2009. A little owl discovers different colors during the day.

Hooray for Fish!
by Lucy Cousins

Here are five *Talkabouts* to use when reading aloud *Hooray for Fish!* to 3-to-5 year olds. Along with the *Talkabouts* are *Follow-Up Fun* activities to do after reading the book.

We suggest following the steps below to help children in this age group develop early literacy concepts and skills as you enjoy the read-aloud experience together.

Step 1 Read *Hooray for Fish!* and the five *Talkabouts* on your own.

Step 2 Select the early literacy concepts and skills that you want to focus on as you read aloud to children.

Step 3 Read aloud *Hooray for Fish!* using appropriate strategies for those concepts and skills.

Step 4 Reread *Hooray for Fish!* at other times using different suggestions in the *Talkabouts.*

Step 5 Choose *Follow-Up Fun* activities to do after reading the book.

Talkabout
Hooray for Fish!

Vocabulary

Before you read the story talk about the cover. You might say:

- The title of this book is ***Hooray for Fish!*** The word *Hooray* is another way to say that you are excited or happy about something. Let's shout the words in the title together— ***Hooray for Fish!*** What colors are the fish on the cover? Are the fish big or little? Let's read the story to find out what the other fish look like.

As you read aloud encourage children to talk about the fish. You might ask:

- Show me the red fish, blue fish, and yellow fish.
- Can you point to the stripy fish? What colors do you see?
- What animal does the ele-fish look like? What do both an elephant and ele-fish have?
- What makes the scary fish look scary? Can you make a scary face?

Positive Parenting Praise! Good job telling about a scary fish.

- What do you see on the sky fish?

Finish reading the story pausing to ask children to tell what their favorite fish in the story looks like.

Talkabout
Hooray for Fish!

Comprehension

Before you read the story talk about the cover. You might say:

- The title of this book is ***Hooray for Fish!*** Let's read the title together—***Hooray for Fish!*** Show me the little fish on the cover. The name of that fish is Little Fish. Point to the big fish. Let's read ***Hooray for Fish!*** to find out about Little Fish and the big fish.

As you read aloud talk about what Little Fish does. You might ask:

- Where does Little Fish live?
- What is Little Fish doing at the beginning of the story?
- Show me how you swim like a fish.

Positive Parenting Praise! Good job swimming like a fish.

- What does Little Fish say to its friends?
- Let's say *Hello* to Little Fish's friends—*Hello, hello!*
- Show me some of Little Fish's friends.
- Which fish does Little Fish love best?

Finish reading the story pausing at the end to ask children to tell who is the big fish on the cover.

Talkabout
Hooray for Fish!

Phonological Awareness

Before you read the story talk about the title. You might say:

- The title of this book is ***Hooray for Fish!*** Say the first word in the title with me—*Hooray.* Listen as I say the word *Hooray* and tap the word parts. (2 taps) Say *Hooray* and tap the word parts with me.

As you read aloud pause to have children listen for the word parts. You might say:

- Listen as I say the word *stripy.* Say the word and tap the word parts with me—*stripy.* (2 taps)
- Listen as I say the words *curly whirly.* Say the words and tap the word parts with me—*curly whirly.* (4 taps)

Positive Parenting Praise! Good job tapping the word parts for *curly whirly.*

Finish reading the story pausing to ask children to join in saying and tapping the word parts—*Hello, hello!* (4 taps)

Talkabout
Hooray for Fish!

Print Concepts.

Before you read the story talk about the title. You might say:

- The title of this book is ***Hooray for Fish!*** Watch as I move my finger under the author's name and read it. Lucy Cousins is the author. She wrote the book. Lucy Cousins is also the illustrator. She drew the pictures in this book.

As you read aloud talk about the space between words. You might say:

- Follow my finger as I move it under the words *hairy fish.*
- Watch as I point to the space between the two words. The space shows where one word ends and the next word begins.
- Follow my finger as I move it under the words *scary fish.*
- Can you show me the space between the two words?

Finish reading the story pausing occasionally to have children point to the space between two words.
Positive Parenting Praise! Good job pointing to the space between two words.

Talkabout
Hooray for Fish!

Letters and Their Sounds

Before you read the story talk about uppercase letter *F* in the title. You might say:

- *Hooray for Fish!* is the name of this book. Listen as I say the word *Fish.* What sound do you hear first in *Fish?* Say the sound with me—*/f/ /f/ /f/.** Uppercase letter *F* stands for the */f/* sound. Point to uppercase letter *F* with me.

Positive Parenting Praise! Good job pointing to uppercase letter *F.*

As you read aloud pause to point to lowercase letter *f* in *fish.* You might say:

- What sound do you hear first in *fish?*
- Say the sound with me—*/f/ /f/ /f/.*
- Lowercase letter *f* stands for the */f/* sound.
- Point to lowercase letter *f* with me.

Finish reading the story pausing occasionally to ask children to say */f/ /f/ /f/* when they hear the word *fish.*

Letter Chant Children can make fish movements with their hands as they chant *f* is for *fish /f/ /f/ f/.*

*The symbol */ /* is used to show the sound a letter stands for. For example, the sound at the beginning of the word *Fish* is the */f/* sound.

Follow-Up Fun
Hooray for Fish!

Act & Play

Let's pretend to be little fish.

Hooray, hooray!
Swim all day.   (wiggle around)
Swim like a happy fish. (smile)
Swim like a sad fish.   (frown)

Hooray, hooray!
Swim all day.   (wiggle around)
Swim like a mad fish.   (stomp feet)
Swim like a scary fish.   (make a scary face)

Swim to the right—*Swim, swim, swim!* (wiggle right)
Swim to the left—*Swim, swim, swim!* (wiggle left)
Hooray, hooray!
Swim all day.
Positive Parenting Praise! Good job swimming like a fish.

Follow-Up Fun
Hooray for Fish!

Say & Sing

One, Two, Three, Four, Five

One, two, three, four, five,   (hold up fingers)
Once I caught a fish alive.

Six, seven, eight, nine, ten,   (hold up fingers)
Then I let it go again.

Why did you let it go?
Because it bit my finger so.

Which finger did it bite?
This little finger on my right. (wigglc littlc fingcr on right hand)

What to Say

- Listen to this rhyme about catching a fish.
- Watch my fingers as I say the rhyme again.
- Let's say the rhyme together using our fingers to show the numbers.

Positive Parenting Praise! Good job wiggling the little finger on your right hand.

Follow-Up Fun
Hooray for Fish!

Draw & Write

Let's make a fish.

What You Need
large paper bags, crayons or markers, newspaper, scissors, stapler

What to Do

1. Cut open a large paper bag. Fold it in half.
2. Draw the outline of a fish. Cut out the two pieces.
3. Staple them together leaving an open space to stuff in newspaper.
4. Have children decorate and name their fish.
5. Write the name of the fish using uppercase letters. Encourage children to identify and trace the letters as they can.

Positive Parenting Praise! Good job tracing the letters.

6. Stuff the newspaper into the fish and staple it closed.
7. Have children swim around the room with their fish.

Follow-Up Fun
Hooray for Fish!

Read Aloud & Enjoy

If your child enjoys *Hooray for Fish!* by Lucy Cousins, we suggest the following book by the same author:

Maisy, Charley, and the Wobbly Tooth by Lucy Cousins, Candlewick, 2006. All of Charley's friends go along with him on his first visit to the dentist.

Here are more books about the ocean and baby animals.

The Deep Blue Sea by Audrey Wood, illustrated by Bruce Wood, Blue Sky Press, 2005. The vivid illustrations show different colors in the deep blue sea.

Kiss Kiss! by Margaret Wild and Bridget Strevens-Marzo, Simon & Schuster, 2003. When Baby Hippo hears animals in the jungle giving their mamas a kiss, he remembers that he forgot to kiss his mama.

Piglet and Mama by Margaret Wild, illustrated by Stephen Michael King, Abrams, 2005. Duck, Horse, Dog, and Sheep try to make Piglet feel better when she cannot find her mama.

Senses at the Seashore by Shelley Rotner, Millbrook, 2006. In this nonfiction book, photographs show children as they see, hear, smell, touch, and taste at the beach.

One Duck Stuck
by Phyllis Root

Here are five *Talkabouts* to use when reading aloud *One Duck Stuck* to 3-to-5 year olds. Along with the *Talkabouts* are *Follow-Up Fun* activities to do after reading the book.

We suggest following the steps below to help children in this age group develop early literacy concepts and skills as you enjoy the read-aloud experience together.

Step 1 Read *One Duck Stuck* and the five *Talkabouts* on your own.

Step 2 Select the early literacy concepts and skills that you want to focus on as you read aloud to children.

Step 3 Read aloud *One Duck Stuck* using appropriate strategies for those concepts and skills.

Step 4 Reread *One Duck Stuck* at other times using different suggestions in the *Talkabouts.*

Step 5 Choose *Follow-Up Fun* activities to do after reading the book.

Talkabout
One Duck Stuck

Vocabulary

Before you read the story talk about the cover. You might say:

- The title of this book is **One Duck Stuck.** Let's say the title together—**One Duck Stuck.** How many ducks do you see on the cover? Let's hold up one finger. Can you point to one duck? I'll point to the word *One.* Let's read the story to listen for number words.

As you read aloud pause to have children identify numbers and number words. You might say:

- This is the number 2.
- How many fish do you see? Count the fish with me—*1, 2.*
- I'll point to the number word *two.* Let's hold up two fingers.

Positive Parenting Praise! Good job holding up two fingers.

- This is the number 3.
- How many moose do you see? Count the moose with me—*1, 2, 3.*
- I'll point to the number word *three.* Let's hold up three fingers.

Finish reading the story pausing to have children point to the numbers and count the animals with you.

Talkabout
One Duck Stuck

Comprehension

Before you read the story talk about the cover. You might say:

- The title of this book is ***One Duck Stuck.*** What animal do you see on the cover? Let's look at its feet. It looks like one foot is stuck. How can you tell? What does the duck want to do? Let's read ***One Duck Stuck*** to find out how the duck gets out of the muck.

As you read aloud pause to encourage children to use the pictures to understand the story. You might ask:

- What do the fish do to help the duck? Is the duck still stuck?
- What do the moose do? Is the duck still stuck?
- How do the frogs try to help? Is the duck stuck?
- How do the skunks try to help? Is the duck still stuck?

Positive Parenting Praise! Good job looking at the pictures to see how the animals try to help.

Finish reading the story pausing to ask children how the duck gets out of the muck and where it goes.

Talkabout
One Duck Stuck

Phonological Awareness

Before you read the story talk about the rhyming words in the title. You might say:

- *One Duck Stuck* is the name of this book. Say the title with me—*One Duck Stuck.* Let's clap the words. (3 claps) Listen as I say the words *Duck* and *Stuck.* The words *Duck* and *Stuck* end with the same sound. *Duck* and *Stuck* rhyme. Say the rhyming words with me—*Duck, Stuck.*

As you read aloud pause to ask children to say rhyming words. You might say:

- Listen as I say the words *duck, stuck, muck.* Say the words with me—*duck, stuck, muck.*
- Do *duck, stuck, muck* end with the same sound? Say the rhyming words with me—*duck, stuck, muck.*
- Listen as I say *No luck. Still stuck.* Listen again and say the two rhyming words with me—*luck, stuck.*

Positive Parenting Praise! Good job saying the rhyming words.

Finish reading the story pausing to ask children to say the missing rhyming word in *No luck. Still_____.*

Talkabout
One Duck Stuck

Print Concepts

Before you read the story talk about the words in the title. You might say:

- The title of this book is ***One Duck Stuck.*** Watch as I move my finger under the words in the title as I read them aloud. Say the words in the title with me—***One Duck Stuck.*** Show me how you move your finger under the words in the title.

As you read aloud pause to show how print is read from left-to-right and top-to-bottom. You might say:

- Watch as I move my finger under the words I read on this page.
- My finger goes from the top of the page to the bottom of the page. Show me the top of the page. Show me the bottom of the page.

Positive Parenting Praise! Good job pointing to the top of the page and the bottom of the page.

- Watch as I move my finger again under the words I read on this page.
- My finger moves from left to right. Show me how you move your finger from left to right under the words.

Finish reading the story pausing to ask children to move their finger under the words *We can! We can!* Encourage children to join in saying the words.

Talkabout
One Duck Stuck

Letters and Their Sounds

Before you read the story talk about uppercase letter *D* in the title. You might say:

- The title of this book is **One Duck Stuck.** Listen as I say the word *Duck.* What sound do you hear first in *Duck?* Say the sound with me—*/d/ /d/ /d/.** Uppercase letter *D* stands for the */d/* sound. Point to uppercase letter *D* with me.

As you read aloud pause to point to lowercase letter *d* in *duck.* You might say:

- What sound do you hear first in *duck?*
- Say the sound with me—*/d/ /d/ /d/.*
- Lowercase letter *d* stands for the */d/* sound.
- Point to lowercase letter *d* with me.

Finish reading the story pausing occasionally to ask children to say */d/ /d/ /d/* when they hear the word *duck.*
Positive Parenting Praise! Good job saying */d/ /d/ /d/* when you hear the word *duck.*

Letter Chant Children can dance as they chant *d* is for *duck /d/ /d/ /d/.*

*The symbol */ /* is used to show the sound a letter stands for. For example, the sound at the beginning of the word *Duck* is the */d/* sound.

Follow-Up Fun
One Duck Stuck

Act & Play

Let's count and move like animals in the story.

Let's count to two—*1, 2.*
Splish like a fish.   (jump)
Splish two times—*1, 2.*

Let's count to three—*1, 2, 3.*
Clomp like a moose.   (stomp feet)
Clomp three times—*1, 2, 3.*
Positive Parenting Praise! Good job counting to three.

Let's count to 9—*1, 2, 3, 4, 5, 6, 7, 8, 9.*
Slink like a snake.   (wiggle on the floor)
Slink nine times—*1, 2, 3, 4, 5, 6, 7, 8, 9.*

Let's count to 10—*1, 2, 3, 4, 5, 6, 7, 8, 9, 10.*
Zing like a dragonfly.   (flap arms)
Zing ten times—*1, 2, 3, 4, 5, 6, 7, 8, 9, 10.*

Follow-Up Fun
One Duck Stuck

Say & Sing

Here Is the Beehive

Here is the beehive.   (make beehive with hands)
Where are all the bees?   (look into beehive)

Hidden away where nobody sees.
Watch and you'll see them,
Come out of the hive.

One, two, three, four, five,   (hold up fingers)
Bzzz Bzzz all fly away!   (flap arms)

What to Say

- Listen to a rhyme about bees and watch as I act it out.
- Let's recite and act out the rhyme together.

Positive Parenting Praise! Good job reciting the rhyme and acting it out.

Follow-Up Fun
One Duck Stuck

Draw & Write

Let's write a counting chart.

What You Need
drawing paper, crayons or markers

What to Do

1. Divide paper into 3 columns and 3 rows.
2. Use a black crayon or marker to write the number *1* in the first column.
3. Write the number word *ONE* in the second column, naming the uppercase letters as you write.
4. Have children choose a different color crayon or marker to draw one line in the third column.

Positive Parenting Praise! Good job drawing one line.

5. Continue filling in the charts with numbers *2* and *3*, encouraging children to draw the appropriate number of lines and trace the numbers as they can.
6. Display their counting charts.

Follow-Up Fun
One Duck Stuck

Read Aloud & Enjoy

If your child enjoys *One Duck Stuck* by Phyllis Root, we suggest the following book by the same author:

Oliver Finds His Way by Phyllis Root, illustrated by Christopher Denise, Candlewick, 2002. Oliver gets lost but finds his way home by listening to the roar of his mama and papa.

Here are more counting books.

Gobble Gobble CRASH! by Julie Stiegemeyer, illustrated by Valeri Gorbachev, Dutton, 2008. This rhyming story tells what four noisy turkeys do during a barnyard counting bash.

In My Garden by Ward Schumaker, Chronicle, 2000. This counting book shows things found in the garden.

ROAR! by Pamela Duncan Edwards, illustrated by Henry Cole, Harper, 2000. A noisy lion cub roars across the African plain looking for playmates in this counting story.

Ten, Nine, Eight by Mary Bang, Greenwillow, 1983. A young child counts down things with her dad in her room before bedtime.

Puffins Climb, Penguins Rhyme
by Bruce McMillan

Here are five *Talkabouts* to use when reading aloud *Puffins Climb, Penguins Rhyme* to 3-to-5 year olds. Along with the *Talkabouts* are *Follow-Up Fun* activities to do after reading the book.

We suggest following the steps below to help children in this age group develop early literacy concepts and skills as you enjoy the read-aloud experience together.

Step 1 Read *Puffins Climb, Penguins Rhyme* and the five *Talkabouts* on your own.

Step 2 Select the early literacy concepts and skills that you want to focus on as you read aloud to children.

Step 3 Read aloud *Puffins Climb, Penguins Rhyme* using appropriate strategies for those concepts and skills.

Step 4 Reread *Puffins Climb, Penguins Rhyme* at other times using different suggestions in the *Talkabouts.*

Step 5 Choose *Follow-Up Fun* activities to do after reading the book.

Talkabout
Puffins Climb, Penguins Rhyme

Vocabulary

Before you read the book talk about the title. You might say:

- The title of this book is **Puffins Climb, Penguins Rhyme.** Say the title with me—**Puffins Climb, Penguins Rhyme.** Let's read the book to listen for words that tell what puffins and penguins do.

As you read aloud have children use the photographs to understand action words. You might say:

- *Groom* means to *clean*. Look at the photograph. What is the penguin using to clean its feathers?

Positive Parenting Praise! Good job using the photograph to learn new words.

- *Squawk* is an animal sound. Let's squawk like a puffin— *Squawk, squawk, squawk!*
- *Brawl* is another word for *fight*. Why are the penguins brawling?
- *Peer* is another word for *look*. Is the puffin peering at a penguin?
- *Glare* means to *look in an angry way*. Why is the penguin angry?

Finish reading the book pausing occasionally to have children demonstrate things penguins and puffins do, such as *stand, fly, eat,* and *walk.*

Talkabout
Puffins Climb, Penguins Rhyme

Comprehension

Before you read the book talk about the birds. You might say:

- The title of this book is *Puffins Climb, Penguins Rhyme.* This book tells about puffins and penguins. Puffins and penguins are birds. What do you know about puffins and penguins? Let's read the book to find out how they look.

As you read aloud encourage children to use the photographs to see how the birds are alike and different. You might say:

- I'll point to a puffin. Can you point to a penguin?
- Are puffins and penguins the same colors?
- I'll point to a puffin's beak. Show me a penguin's beak.
- Are their beaks the same color?

Positive Parenting Praise! Good job using pictures in the book to learn about puffins and penguins.

Finish reading the book pausing occasionally before reading a page to ask children if they see a puffin or penguin in the photograph.

Talkabout
Puffins Climb, Penguins Rhyme
Phonological Awareness

Before you read the book talk about rhyming words. You might say:

- The name of this book is ***Puffins Climb, Penguins Rhyme.*** Say the title with me—***Puffins Climb, Penguins Rhyme.*** Listen as I say the word *Climb.* What word in the title rhymes with *Climb?* Let's say the rhyming words together—*Climb, Rhyme.*

As you read aloud pause to have children rhyme one word with another. You might say:

- Listen for rhyming words as I read about puffins. What word rhymes with *land?*
- *Land* and *stand* rhyme. Say the rhyming words with me—*land, stand.*
- Listen for rhyming words as I read about penguins. What word rhymes with *groom?*
- *Groom* and *zoom* rhyme. Say the rhyming words with me—*groom, zoom.*

Positive Parenting Praise! Good job saying rhyming words.

Finish reading the book pausing to ask children to join in saying rhyming words.

Talkabout
Puffins Climb, Penguins Rhyme

Print Concepts

Before you read the book talk about the title. You might say:

- The title of this book is *Puffins Climb, Penguins Rhyme.* Watch as I move my finger under the words in the title. Say the words with me—*Puffins Climb, Penguins Rhyme.* Show me how you move your finger under the words in the title.

As you read aloud help children understand that sentences are made up of words. You might say:

- Watch my finger as I move it under the words as I read the sentence *Puffins land.*
- Say the sentence with me—*Puffins land.*
- I'll point to the first word in the sentence. Now look as I point to the last word in the sentence. Show me the space between the two words.

Positive Parenting Praise! Good job pointing to the space between the two words.

- The dot at the end of the sentence is a period. It shows where to stop reading.

Finish reading the book pausing several times to have children point to the first word and the last word in a sentence.

Talkabout

Puffins Climb, Penguins Rhyme

Letters and Their Sounds

Before you read the book talk about uppercase letter *P* in the title. You might say:

- The title of this book is **Puffins Climb, Penguins Rhyme**. Listen as I say the word *Puffins*. What sound do you hear first in *Puffins*? Say the sound with me—/p/ /p/ /p/.* Uppercase letter *P* stands for the /p/ sound. Point to uppercase letter *P* with me.

As you read aloud pause to point to lowercase letter *p* in *peer*. You might say:

- What sound do you hear first in *peer*?
- Say the sound with me—/p/ /p/ /p/.

Positive Parenting Praise! Good job saying the first sound you hear in the word *peer*.

- Lowercase letter *p* stands for the /p/ sound.
- Point to lowercase letter *p* with me.

Finish reading the book pausing for children to say /p/ /p/ /p/ when they hear the words *puffins* and *penguins*.

Letter Chant Children can parade around like puffins and penguins as they chant *P* is for *Puffins* /p/ /p/ /p/, *P* is for *Penguins* /p/ /p/ /p/.

*The symbol // is used to show the sound a letter stands for. For example, the sound at the beginning of the word *Puffins* is the /p/ sound.

Follow-Up Fun
Puffins Climb, Penguins Rhyme

Act & Play

Let's pretend to be puffins and penguins.

I am a puffin.
I like to walk and squawk.   (walk and squawk)
I am a puffin.
I like to glide and hide.   (glide and hide)
I am a puffin.
Positive Parenting Praise! Good job gliding and hiding like a puffin.

I am a penguin.
I like to hop and stop.   (hop and stop)
I am a penguin.
I like to groom and zoom. (groom and zoom)
I am a penguin.

Follow-Up Fun
Puffins Climb, Penguins Rhyme

Say & Sing

Once I Saw a Little Bird

Once I saw a little bird   (flap arms)
Come hop, hop, hop.   (hop)
So I cried, "Little bird,
Will you stop, stop, stop?"   (hold up hand)

And I was going to the window
To say, "How do you do?"   (wave hand)
But he shook his little tail,   (shake tail)
And away he flew.   (fly away)

What to Say

- Listen to this rhyme about a little bird.
- Let's say the rhyme together and act out what a little bird does.
- Listen to the rhyme again and fill in the missing rhyming words. *(hop, stop; do, flew)*

Positive Parenting Praise! Good job saying the rhyming words.

Follow-Up Fun
Puffins Climb, Penguins Rhyme

Draw & Write

Let's write a book about penguins.

What You Need
drawing paper, crayons or markers

What to Do

1. Fold paper in half.
2. Write the title *PENGUINS* on the cover using uppercase letters, naming the letters as you write.
3. Read the title. Have children say the title.
4. Ask children to tell what penguins look like and what they like to do.
5. Record their responses on the inside pages. Move your finger under the words as you read them.

Positive Parenting Praise! Good job telling what penguins look like.

6. Have children draw pictures of penguins in their books.
7. Display their books so children can look at them.

Follow-Up Fun
Puffins Climb, Penguins Rhyme

Read Aloud & Enjoy

If your child enjoys *Puffins Climb, Penguins Rhyme* by Bruce McMillan, we suggest the following book by the same author:

Kitten Can . . . by Bruce McMillan, Lothrop, 1984. Photographs and text show things that a kitten can do.

Here are more nonfiction and animal books.

Bread Bread Bread by Ann Morris, photographs by Ken Heyman, Harper, 1989. Photographs and words tell about the breads people eat in different places around the world.

Do Donkeys Dance? by Melanie Walsh, Houghton, 2000. In question-and-answer format, children learn about things animals can and cannot do.

If You Were a Penguin by Wendell and Florence Minor, Harper, 2009. Simple text and illustrations explain things that penguins do.

Why Do Kittens PURR? by Marion Dane Bauer, illustrated by Henry Cole, Simon & Schuster, 2003. Questions are asked about things animals do and answers are given in rhyming text.

Sheep in a Jeep

by Nancy Shaw

Here are five **Talkabouts** to use when reading aloud **Sheep in a Jeep** to 3-to-5 year olds. Along with the **Talkabouts** are **Follow-Up Fun** activities to do after reading the book.

We suggest following the steps below to help children in this age group develop early literacy concepts and skills as you enjoy the read-aloud experience together.

Step 1 Read **Sheep in a Jeep** and the five **Talkabouts** on your own.

Step 2 Select the early literacy concepts and skills that you want to focus on as you read aloud to children.

Step 3 Read aloud **Sheep in a Jeep** using appropriate strategies for those concepts and skills.

Step 4 Reread **Sheep in a Jeep** at other times using different suggestions in the **Talkabouts.**

Step 5 Choose **Follow-Up Fun** activities to do after reading the book.

Talkabout
Sheep in a Jeep

Vocabulary

Before you read the story talk about the title. You might say:

- The name of this book is ***Sheep in a Jeep.*** Can you point to the sheep? Show me the jeep. Who is driving the jeep? What are the other sheep doing? Let's read the story to listen for words that tell what the sheep do.

As you read aloud pause to talk about action words. You might say:

- See the sheep leap. Show me how you leap.
- See the sheep shove the jeep. Can you pretend to shove a jeep?
- The sheep shrug. Watch me shrug as I move my shoulders up and down. Let's shrug our shoulders together.
- The sheep shout when the jeep comes out of the mud. Let's shout for the sheep—*Hooray!*
- The jeep is in a heap so the sheep weep. Show me how you weep like a sad, sad sheep.

Positive Parenting Praise! Good job weeping like a sheep.

Finish reading the story encouraging children to act out sweeping the heap of jeep parts.

Talkabout
Sheep in a Jeep

Comprehension

Before you read the story talk about the cover. You might say:

- The title of this book is ***Sheep in a Jeep.*** The picture on the cover tells about the story. What are the sheep riding in? What might happen to the jeep? Let's read ***Sheep in a Jeep*** to find out what happens.

As you read aloud pause to have children make predictions about what might happen. You might ask:

- What will the sheep do to make the jeep go up the hill?
- If the sheep don't look, what might happen to the jeep?
- Where does the jeep get stuck?
- What animals help the sheep? How can the pigs help?
- If the driver forgets to steer, what might happen to the jeep?

Finish reading the story pausing to talk with children about what happens to the jeep.
Positive Parenting Praise! Good job telling about the jeep at the end of the story.

Talkabout
Sheep in a Jeep

Phonological Awareness

Before you read the story talk about rhyming words. You might say:

- *Sheep in a Jeep* is the title of this book. Say the words in the title with me—***Sheep in a Jeep.*** The words *Sheep* and *Jeep* both end with the same sound. *Sheep* and *jeep* rhyme. Say the rhyming words with me—*Sheep, Jeep.*

As you read aloud talk about and listen for rhyming words. You might say:

- Listen as I say the words—*beep, sheep, jeep, steep.* The words end with the same sound. The words *beep, sheep, jeep, steep* rhyme. Say and clap the rhyming words with me—*beep, sheep, jeep, steep.* (4 claps)
- Listen as I say the words—*leap, jeep.* Do the words end with the same sound? The words *leap* and *jeep* rhyme. Say and clap the rhyming words with me—*leap, jeep.* (2 claps)

Positive Parenting Praise! Good job saying and clapping the rhyming words.

Finish reading the story encouraging children to say and clap the rhyming words, such as *grunt/front, thud/mud, tug/shrug, yelp/help, out/shout, cheer/steer, heap/sweep,* and *weep/cheap.*

Talkabout
Sheep in a Jeep

Print Concepts

Before you read the story talk about the author and illustrator. You might say:

- The title of this book is **Sheep in a Jeep.** The author is Nancy Shaw. She wrote the story. The illustrator is Margot Apple. She drew the pictures. The words and pictures tell the story.

As you read aloud pause occasionally to point out where to begin and end reading words on a page. You might say:

- Watch as I point to where to begin reading the words on this page.
- Show me where to begin reading the words on the next page.

Positive Parenting Praise! Good job showing where to begin reading.

- Watch as I point to where to stop reading on this page. The period shows where to stop. The period is at the end of a sentence.
- Show me where to stop reading the words on the next page.

Finish reading the story pausing occasionally to have children point to where sentences begin and end on a page.

Talkabout
Sheep in a Jeep

Letters and Their Sounds

Before you read the story talk about uppercase letter *J* in the title. You might say:

- The title of this book is ***Sheep in a Jeep.*** Listen as I say the word *Jeep*. What sound do you hear first in *Jeep?* Say the sound with me—*/j/ /j/ /j/.* * Uppercase letter *J* stands for the */j/* sound. Point to uppercase letter *J* with me.

Positive Parenting Praise! Good job saying the */j/* sound and pointing to uppercase letter *J*.

As you read aloud pause to point to lowercase letter *j* in *jeep*. You might say:

- What sound do you hear first in *jeep?*
- Say the sound with me—*/j/ /j/ /j/.*
- Lowercase letter *j* stands for the */j/* sound.
- Point to lowercase letter *j* with me.

Finish reading the story pausing occasionally to ask children to say */j/ /j/ /j/* when they hear the word *jeep*.

Letter Chant Children can jog in a circle as they chant *J is for Jeep /j/ /j/ /j/.*

*The symbol // is used to show the sound a letter stands for. For example, the sound at the beginning of the word *Jeep* is the */j/* sound.

Follow-Up Fun
Sheep in a Jeep

Act & Play

Let's pretend to ride with a sheep and other animals in a jeep.

A sheep drives a jeep.   (hold a steering wheel)
Jiggety-jeepity, jiggety-jeepity.   (bounce up and down)

A toad on the road hops into the jeep.   (hop)
A pig in a wig jumps into the jeep.   (jump)

A fox with a pie in a box leaps into the jeep.   (leap)
Jiggety-jeepity, jiggety-jeepity.   (bounce up and down)

Oh me! Oh my!   (place hands on cheeks)
I see a fly on the pie!   (point finger)

Buzz, buzz, buzz—jiggety-jeepity. (bounce up and down)
Stop, sheep, stop!   (hold up hand)
Positive Parenting Praise! Good job pretending to ride in a jeep.

Follow-Up Fun
Sheep in a Jeep

Say & Sing

Baa, Baa, Black Sheep

Baa, baa, black sheep,
Have you any wool?
Yes, sir, yes, sir,
Three bags full;   (hold up three fingers)

One for my master,   (hold up one finger)
And one for the dame,   (hold up two fingers)
And one for the little boy   (hold up three fingers)
Who lives down the lane.

What to Say

- Listen to the rhyme "Baa, Baa, Black Sheep."
- Let's recite the rhyme together.

Positive Parenting Praise! Good job reciting the rhyme.

- Let's recite the rhyme again using our fingers to show the numbers.

Follow-Up Fun
Sheep in a Jeep

Draw & Write

Let's write a sign for a jeep.

What You Need
construction paper, crayons or markers

What to Do

1. Write *JEEP FOR SALE* on paper. Name the uppercase letters as you write them. Move your finger under the words as you read them.
2. Ask children to point to the spaces between the words.
3. Have children draw pictures on their signs.
4. Encourage children to tell about their pictures. Record their responses on their pictures.

Positive Parenting Praise! Good job telling about your picture.

5. Display their *JEEP FOR SALE* signs.

Follow-Up Fun
Sheep in a Jeep

Read Aloud & Enjoy

If your child enjoys *Sheep in a Jeep* by Nancy Shaw and illustrated by Margot Apple, we suggest the following book by the same author and illustrator:

Sheep Take a Hike by Nancy Shaw, illustrated by Margot Apple, Houghton, 1994. A group of sheep takes a hike in the woods.

Here are more books about animals and things that go.

Beep, Beep, Let's Go! by Eleanor Taylor, Bloomsbury, 2005. Animals use various means of transportation to go to the beach.

Duck in the Truck by Jez Alborough, Harper, 1999. Duck's friends try to get his truck out of the muck where it is stuck.

There's a Cow in the Cabbage Patch by Clare Beaton, illustrated by Stella Blackstone, Barefoot, 2001. Animals on a farm are in the wrong places until dinnertime when they go back to where they belong.

Where Is the Green Sheep? by Mem Fox, illustrated by Judy Horacek, Harcourt, 2004. Whimsical illustrations and repetitive text tell about different sheep that can be seen before the green sheep is finally found.

The Snowy Day
by Ezra Jack Keats

Here are five *Talkabouts* to use when reading aloud *The Snowy Day* to 3-to-5 year olds. Along with the *Talkabouts* are *Follow-Up Fun* activities to do after reading the book.

We suggest following the steps below to help children in this age group develop early literacy concepts and skills as you enjoy the read-aloud experience together.

Step 1   Read *The Snowy Day* and the five *Talkabouts* on your own.

Step 2   Select the early literacy concepts and skills that you want to focus on as you read aloud to children.

Step 3   Read aloud *The Snowy Day* using appropriate strategies for those concepts and skills.

Step 4   Reread *The Snowy Day* at other times using different suggestions in the *Talkabouts.*

Step 5   Choose *Follow-Up Fun* activities to do after reading the book.

Talkabout
The Snowy Day

Vocabulary

Before you read the story talk about the cover. You might say:

- The title of this book is **_The Snowy Day._** Let's say the title together—**_The Snowy Day._** Look at the picture on the cover. Is it day or night? Let's read **_The Snowy Day_** to listen for words that tell about things that happen during the day and at night.

As you read aloud pause to help children understand words related to time. You might ask:

- Does Peter eat breakfast in the morning or at night?
- Is morning at the beginning or the end of the day?
- What does Peter put in his pocket at the end of the day?
- What does Peter do before bedtime?

Positive Parenting Praise! Good job telling what Peter does before bedtime.

- Is bedtime in the morning or at night?
- What do you do before going to bed at night?

Finish reading the story pausing to ask children to tell what Peter and his friend will do after breakfast the next morning.

Talkabout
The Snowy Day

Comprehension

Before you read the story talk about the cover. You might say:

- *The Snowy Day* is the title of this book. Let's say the title together—*The Snowy Day.* Can you point to the boy in the picture on the cover. Is the boy inside or outside? What is he wearing? What is he doing? Let's read the story to find out what the boy does on a snowy day.

As you read aloud talk about the story character, setting, and events. You might ask:

- What does Peter see out the window when he wakes up?
- How does Peter make tracks in the snow?
- How does Peter make a snow angel? Show me how you make a snow angel.

Positive Parenting Praise! Good job showing how you make a snow angel.

- Does Peter like to play outside in the snow?
- Where does Peter go after playing outside?

Finish reading the story pausing to talk about what happens to the snowball in Peter's pocket.

Talkabout
The Snowy Day

Phonological Awareness

Before you read the story talk about the title. You might say:

- The name of this book is **The Snowy Day.** This story is about a boy named Peter. Listen as I say the name *Peter.* What sound do you hear first in the name *Peter?*

As you read aloud pause to have children identify beginning sounds they hear in words. You might say:

- Peter uses his feet to make footprints in the snow. Listen as I say the word *feet.* What sound do you hear first in *feet?*

Positive Parenting Praise! Good job listening for the first sound you hear in *feet.*

- Peter uses his hand to hold a stick. Listen as I say the word *hand.* What sound do you hear first in *hand?*
- Peter puts a snowball in his pocket. Listen as I say the word *pocket.* What sound do you hear first in *pocket?*

Finish reading the story encouraging children to listen for the beginning sounds in the words *house, socks, sun,* and *bed.*

Talkabout
The Snowy Day

Print Concepts

Before you read the story talk about the title. You might say:

- The title of this book is *The Snowy Day.* The title is the name of the book. Ezra Jack Keats is the author and illustrator. He wrote the story and drew the pictures. The words and pictures tell about a snowy day.

As you read aloud pause several times to point out where to begin reading on a page. You might say:

- Look at the words on this page. Watch as I point to where to begin reading on the page.
- Watch as I move my finger under the words as I read them.
- Look at the words on the next page. Show me where to begin reading the words on the page.

Positive Parenting Praise! Good job showing where to begin reading on a page.

- Show me how you move your finger under the words as I read on the next page.

Finish reading the story pausing on the last page to point out where to begin reading on the page and where the story ends.

Talkabout
The Snowy Day

Letters and Their Sounds

Before you read the story talk about uppercase letter *D* in the title. You might say:

- The title of this book is **The Snowy Day.** Listen as I say the word *Day.* What sound do you hear first in *Day?* Say the sound with me—/d/ /d/ /d/.* Uppercase letter *D* stands for the /d/ sound. Point to uppercase letter *D* with me.

As you read aloud pause to point to lowercase letter *d* in the word *down.* You might say:

- What sound do you hear first in *down?*
- Say the sound with me—/d/ /d/ /d/.
- Lowercase letter *d* stands for the /d/ sound.
- Point to lowercase letter *d* with me.

Finish reading the story pausing at the end to ask children to listen for the first sound they hear in the word *deep.*
Positive Parenting Praise! Good job saying /d/ /d/ /d/ when you hear the word *deep.*

Letter Chant Children can bend down as they chant *d* is for *down* /d/ /d/ /d/.

*The symbol / / is used to show the sound a letter stands for. For example, the sound at the beginning of the word *Day* is the /d/ sound.

Follow-Up Fun
The Snowy Day

Act & Play

Let's pretend to play outside on a snowy day.

Let's put on a snowsuit, a hat, two boots, two mittens, and a scarf.
Now let's walk slowly in the snow—*Crunch, crunch, crunch!*

Next, let's stomp in the deep snow—*Stomp, stomp, stomp!*
Let's make a snowball—*Toss, toss, toss!*

What else can we do in the snow?
Let's use a shovel—*Dig, dig, dig!*
And make a pile of snow—*Big, big, big!*
Positive Parenting Praise! Good job making a big pile of snow.

On a snowy, blowy day,   (say *Brrr*)
My hat wants to blow away! (put hand on top of head)

Follow-Up Fun
The Snowy Day

Say & Sing

The Snowflake Man

Do you know the snowflake man, (7 taps)
The snowflake man, the snowflake man? (8 taps)
Do you know the snowflake man (7 taps)
Who lives on Snowball Lane? (6 taps)

Yes, I know the snowflake man, (7 taps)
The snowflake man, the snowflake man. (8 taps)
Yes, I know the snowflake man (7 taps)
Who lives on Snowball Lane. (6 taps)

What to Say

- Listen as I sing a song about a snowflake man. (Sing the song to the tune of "The Muffin Man.")

Positive Parenting Praise! Good job listening to the song.

- Sing the song with me.
- Let's sing the song again and tap the word parts together.

Follow-Up Fun
The Snowy Day

Draw & Write

Let's make a pair of mittens.

What You Need
drawing paper, crayons or markers, scissors, string, stapler

What to Do

1. Draw an outline of a pair of mittens on the paper.
2. Have children decorate their mittens.

Positive Parenting Praise! Good job drawing stripes on your mittens.

3. Use uppercase letters to write children's names on their mittens. Children can trace the letters in their names.
4. Cut out the mittens and attach them together by stapling on string.
5. Display children's mittens.

Follow-Up Fun
The Snowy Day

Read Aloud & Enjoy

If your child enjoys *The Snowy Day* by Ezra Jack Keats, we suggest the following book by the same author:

Whistle for Willie by Ezra Jack Keats, Viking, 1964. Learning how to whistle helps Peter find his dog Willie.

Here are more books about seasons.

Bear in Sunshine by Stella Blackstone, illustrated by Debbie Harter, Barefoot, 2001. Bear finds fun things to do in all seasons.

The First Day of Winter by Denise Fleming, Holt, 2005. Colorful illustrations tell about a snowman that takes ten days to build.

Leaf Man by Lois Ehlert, Harcourt, 2005. Large illustrations of autumn leaves show the path that Leaf Man takes as the wind blows.

Summer Wonders by Bill Raczka, illustrated by Judy Stead, Whitman, 2009. Simple text and illustrations tell about things people do during the summer.

PART III

READ-ALOUD BOOKS ON FAVORITE TOPICS AND MORE *FOLLOW-UP FUN* ACTIVITIES

In Part III, there are books to read aloud and *Follow-Up Fun* activities to do with children during their first five years to develop early literacy concepts and skills and their love of books and learning. These books cover a range of favorite children's topics. The *Follow-Up Fun* activities are easily adaptable to use with these books, or any books suitable for young children. You can refer to the Appendix for additional book titles.

6

ALL ABOUT ME

Before you read aloud one of the books listed below, preview the book and choose strategies modeled in the *Talkabouts* to support the development of early literacy concepts and skills.

All by Myself! by Aliki, Harper, 2000. Illustrations and simple text show things a young child learns to do.

The Handiest Thing in the World by Andrew Clements, photographs by Raquel Jaramillo, Atheneum, 2010. Photographs of young children show them using their hands to do many things, such as playing with a dog, using a calculator, and catching butterflies.

Mice Squeak, We Speak by Tomie dePaola, Penguin, 1997. This book introduces children to the sounds animals make and the words people use in a rhyming poem by Arnold L. Shapiro.

A Rainbow All Around Me by Sandra L. Pinkney, photographs by Myles C. Pinkney, Cartwheel, 2002. Children from different ethnic groups are shown with colors all around them.

Ten Little Fingers and Ten Little Toes by Mem Fox, illustrated by Helen Oxenbury, Harcourt, 2008. Rhyming text and illustrations of babies born in different places around the world tell how children are all alike.

Follow-Up Fun
All About Me

Act & Play

Let's act out things you do in the morning.
I stretch when I get out of bed.
I brush my teeth.
I eat breakfast.
I put on my clothes.
Positive Parenting Praise! Good job pretending that you are getting dressed.

Let's act out things you do in the afternoon.
I run very fast.
I skip in a circle.
I hop in a line.
I draw a picture.

Let's act out things you do at night.
I put on my pajamas.
I listen to a story.
I brush my teeth.
I go to bed.

Follow-Up Fun
All About Me

Say & Sing

If You're Happy and You Know It

If you're happy and you know it,
Clap your hands.   (clap)
If you're happy and you know it,
Clap your hands.   (clap)
If you're happy and you know it,
And you really want to show it,
If you're happy and you know it,
Clap your hands.   (clap)
Positive Parenting Praise! Good job clapping your hands.

What to Say

- Listen as I sing a song and watch what I do with my hands.
- Let's sing the song and clap our hands together.
- Let's sing the song again and tap our shoulders.
- Let's sing it another time and touch our toes.

Follow-Up Fun
All About Me

Draw & Write

Let's draw a face.

What You Need
paper plate, crayons or markers, craft sticks, tape

What to Do

1. Have children draw eyes, a nose, a mouth, and hair on a paper plate.

Positive Parenting Praise! Good job drawing a face on the plate.

2. Write children's names using uppercase letters on the plate.
3. Have children name and trace the letters as they can.
4. Use tape to attach a craft stick to the back of the plate.
5. Have children hold up their plates as they go around introducing themselves by saying *My name is* (child's name).

7

FAMILIES AND FRIENDS

Before you read aloud one of the books listed below, preview the book and choose strategies modeled in the *Talkabouts* to support the development of early literacy concepts and skills.

Bear's Busy Family by Stella Blackstone, illustrated by Debbie Harter, Barefoot, 2000. A young bear introduces family members by telling special things they do.

City Dog, Country Frog by Mo Willems, illustrated by Jon J. Muth, Hyperion, 2010. This story is about the friendship between a dog and frog during different seasons of the year.

Owl Babies by Martin Waddell, illustrated by Patrick Benson, Candlewick, 1972. Three baby owls worry while their mother is away and are happy when she returns.

This Way, Ruby! by Jonathan Emmett, illustrated by Rebecca Harry, Scholastic, 2007. Ruby's siblings lose their way back home, but she shows them where to go.

We're Going on a Bear Hunt! by Michael Rosen, illustrated by Helen Oxenbury, McElderry, 1989. A family joins together on an adventure to find a bear.

Follow-Up Fun
Families and Friends

Act & Play

Let's pretend to go on a family picnic.

Stop the car. Here we are.   (hand up)
Let's carry the food basket. (carry basket)
Let's spread the blanket on the grass. (spread blanket)
Sit down.   (sit)

Let's eat a sandwich—*Munch, munch, munch!*
Let's eat an apple—*Crunch, crunch, crunch!*
Let's play catch.   (throw and catch)
Positive Parenting Praise! Good job pretending to throw and catch a ball.

Let's take a walk.   (walk around)
Let's eat an ice cream.   (lick an ice cream cone)
Let's take a nap. (rest head on hands)

Follow-Up Fun
Families and Friends

Say & Sing

Welcome Friends
One, two,   (hold up two fingers)
I know you!

Three, four,   (hold up four fingers)
Here come more!

Five, six,   (hold up six fingers)
No tricks!
Positive Parenting Praise! Good job holding up your six fingers.

Seven, eight,   (hold up eight fingers)
You are late!

Nine, ten,   (hold up ten fingers)
Welcome friends!

What to Say

- Listen and watch as I recite a rhyme.
- Let's say the rhyme together and hold up our fingers to show the numbers.
- Let's say the rhyme again and wave to our friends at the end.

Follow-Up Fun
Families and Friends

Draw & Write

Let's write a story about your family.

What You Need
drawing paper, crayons or markers

What to Do

1. Fold the paper in half.
2. Use uppercase letters to write MY FAMILY on the cover. Read the words and ask children to say them with you.
3. Have children draw pictures of family members on the inside pages.
4. As children name the family members, use uppercase letters to label each person.

Positive Parenting Praise! Good job drawing your family members.

5. Display their books.

8

FOODS

Before you read aloud one of the books listed below, preview the book and choose strategies modeled in the *Talkabouts* to support the development of early literacy concepts and skills.

Bee-bim Bop! by Linda Sue Park, illustrated by Ho Baek Lee, Clarion, 2005. A young girl helps her mom shop so they can cook a favorite dish for their family.

The Carrot Seed by Ruth Krauss, illustrated by Crockett Johnson, HarperCollins, 1945. In this classic, a young boy plants a carrot seed and watches it grow into a huge carrot.

Feast for 10 by Cathryn Falwell, Clarion, New York, 1993. Counting from 1 to 10 and back again, a family takes part in shopping for groceries, preparing the food, and sharing in a feast.

Growing Vegetable Soup by Lois Ehlert, Harcourt, 1987. After planting a vegetable garden together, a father and child make soup using the vegetables.

Pigs Love Potatoes by Anika Denise, illustrated by Christopher Denise, Philomel, 2007. In this counting book, a mother pig cooks potatoes for her family.

Follow-Up Fun
Foods

Act & Play

Let's pretend to work in a garden.

A rake, a shovel, a hoe. (hold a tool)
It's off to the garden we go. (walk around the room)

We plant sprouts and seeds. (kneel down and dig)
Lots of water the garden needs. (water garden)
Positive Parenting Praise! Good job watering the plants.

We watch our vegetables grow. (point to eyes)
They'll be yummy to eat we know. (pat tummies)

Follow-Up Fun
Foods

The Snail and the Mouse

Slowly, slowly, very slowly   (move fingers slowly)
Goes the garden snail.

Slowly, slowly, very slowly
Up the garden rail.   (move fingers up slowly)

Quickly, quickly, very quickly   (move feet quickly)
Runs the little mouse.

Quickly, quickly, very quickly   (move feet quickly)
To its little house.   (cup hands together)
Positive Parenting Praise! Good job being a snail and a mouse.

What to Say

- Listen to a rhyme about a snail and a little mouse in a garden.
- Listen again and join in the words and actions.
- What are some vegetables that might grow in the garden?

Follow-Up Fun
Foods

Draw & Write

Let's draw and label vegetables.

What You Need
paper plates, crayons or markers

What to Do

1. Have children draw a picture of a vegetable that they like to eat on their plates. Ask children to name the vegetable.
2. Repeat the vegetable name and have children listen for and say the first sound in the word.
3. Name the letter the sound stands for. For example: The letter *t* stands for /t/. The word *tomato* begins with *t*.

Positive Parenting Praise! Good job listening for the first sound in the word *tomato*.

4. Write the vegetable name on the plate, using uppercase letters, and naming the letters as you write.
5. Display their vegetable plates.

9

ANIMALS

Before you read aloud one of the books listed below, preview the book and choose strategies modeled in the *Talkabouts* to support the development of early literacy concepts and skills.

Brown Bear, Brown Bear, What Do You See? by Bill Martin Jr, illustrated by Eric Carle, Holt, 1983. Brown Bear and other colorful animals answer the question posed in the book title.

Chicken Little by Rebecca Emberley and Ed Emberley, Roaring Brook Press, 2009. Large colorful illustrations and text tell a funny version of this classic children's story.

The Cow Loves Cookies by Karma Wilson, illustrated by Marcellus Hall, McElderry, 2010. Animals on a farm love eating their own foods, but an unusual cow loves eating cookies in this humorous story.

Duck! Rabbit! by Amy Krouse Rosenthal & Tom Lichtenheld, Chronicle Books, 2009. Using picture clues, young children try to figure out whether the animal in the book is a duck or a rabbit.

Off We Go! by Jane Yolen, illustrated by Laurel Molk, Little, Brown, 2000. Baby animals sing on their way to Grandma's house.

Follow-Up Fun
Animals

Act & Play

Let's pretend to be animals.

Let's be black cats—*Meow, meow, meow!*
Stretch like a cat.   (stretch arms)
Point to things that are black.

Let's be blue birds—*Chirp, chirp, chirp!*
Fly like a bird.   (flap arms)
Point to things that are blue.

Let's be green frogs—*Croak, croak, croak!*
Leap like a frog.   (leap)
Point to things that are green.
Positive Parenting Praise! Good job finding things that are green.

Let's be brown dogs—*Woof, woof, woof!*
Sniff like a dog.   (sniff)
Point to things that are brown.

Follow-Up Fun
Animals

Say & Sing

Teddy Bear, Teddy Bear

Teddy Bear, Teddy Bear,
Turn around.   (turn around)
Teddy Bear, Teddy Bear,
Touch the ground.   (touch the floor)
Teddy Bear, Teddy Bear,
Tie your shoe.   (point to shoe)
Teddy Bear, Teddy Bear,
That will do.   (clap)

What to Say

- Listen and watch as I recite the rhyme.
- Let's say the rhyme and act it out together.

Positive Parenting Praise! Good job acting out the rhyme.

- Let's say the rhyme again and do others things, such as shake our heads, pat our shoulders, and touch our knees.

Follow-Up Fun
Animals

Draw & Write

Let's make an animal mobile.

What You Need
wire hangers, crayons or markers, index cards, string, hole punch

What to Do

1. Draw outlines of children's favorite animals on index cards.
2. Have children color their animals.

Positive Parenting Praise! Good job coloring the horse brown.

3. Write the name of each animal on the cards using upper-case letters. Name the letters as you write.
4. Punch a hole at the top of each index card. Attach a piece of string to each card. Tie strings to the hangers.
5. Display their mobiles.

10

DINOSAURS

Before you read aloud one of the books listed below, preview the book and choose strategies modeled in the *Talkabouts* to support the development of early literacy concepts and skills.

Dino-Pets by Lynn Plourde, illustrated by Gideon Kendall, Dutton, 2007. Large colorful illustrations of dinosaurs and repetitive rhyming text tell about a boy who has different kinds of dinosaurs as pets.

Dinosaur Dinosaur by Kevin Lewis, illustrated by Daniel Kirk, Orchard, 2006. A dinosaur keeps busy all day long.

Dinosaurs, Dinosaurs by Byron Barton, HarperCollins, 1989. Illustrations help children learn about dinosaurs that roamed around long ago.

How Do Dinosaurs Say Good Night? by Jane Yolen, illustrated by Mark Teague, Blue Sky, 2000. The rhyming text asks and answers questions about dinosaurs' bedtime behavior.

Sammy and the Dinosaurs by Ian Whybrow, illustrated by Adrian Reynolds, Orchard Books, 1999. A little boy named Sammy discovers toy dinosaurs in his grandmother's attic.

Follow-Up Fun
Dinosaurs

Act & Play

Let's pretend to be dinosaurs.

I am a dinosaur.
Listen to me roar—*ROAR!*

I am big and strong.   (show muscles)
I chomp and I stomp.   (move jaws, stomp feet)
Positive Parenting Praise! Good job being a big and strong dinosaur.

I wiggle and I giggle.   (shake, giggle)
I walk and I talk.   (take giant steps, make dinosaur sounds)

I read and I sing.   (hold a book, sing)
I dance and I clap.   (dance, clap)

I am a dinosaur.
Listen to me roar—*ROAR!*

Follow-Up Fun
Dinosaurs

Say & Sing

Dinosaur Dinosaur

Dinosaur Dinosaur
Runs through the town,   (run in place)
Upstairs, downstairs   (hands up, hands down)
In a nightgown.
Rapping at the windows,   (knock)
Roaring through the locks,   (roar)
"Are the baby dinosaurs all in bed?
For now it's eight o'clock!" (hold up 8 fingers)

What to Say

- Listen to a rhyme about a dinosaur.

Positive Parenting Praise! Good job listening to the rhyme.

- Let's say the rhyme and act it out together.

Follow-Up Fun
Dinosaurs

Draw & Write

Let's write a dinosaur birthday card.

What You Need
drawing paper, crayons or markers

What to Do

1. Fold the paper in half.
2. Have children draw a picture of a dinosaur on the front of the card.

Positive Parenting Praise! Good job drawing a picture of a dinosaur.

3. Write *Happy Birthday* on the inside of the card. Name the letters as you write.
4. Have children write their names as they can.
5. Display their birthday cards.

11

THINGS THAT GO

Before you read aloud one of the books listed below, preview the book and choose strategies modeled in the *Talkabouts* to support the development of early literacy concepts and skills.

Little Blue Truck Leads the Way by Alice Schertle, illustrated by Jill McEmurry, Houghton Mifflin Harcourt, 2009. A little blue drives in the city where there are lots of big trucks around.

Melvin might? by Jon Scieszka, illustrated by David Shannon, Loren Long, and David Gordon, Simon & Schuster, 2008. A cement mixer named Melvin saves his ambulance friend Rescue Rita.

School Bus by Donald Crews, Morrow, 1993. Using few words and many illustrations of yellow buses, this book shows children being taken to school and returning back home at day's end.

Tip Tip Dig Dig by Emma Garcia, Boxer, 2007. Simple text combines with illustrations of construction vehicles to describe the work they do to build an adventure playground.

A Train Goes Clickety-Clack by Jonathan London, illustrated by Denis Roche, Holt, 2007. Colorful illustrations and simple rhyming text make the train ride seem real to young children.

Follow-Up Fun
Things That Go

Act & Play

Let's pretend to be fire trucks.

I'm a little fire engine hear me say—*Whoo, whoo, whoo!*
Get out of my way!

I turn to the right—*Zoom, zoom, zoom!*   (move right)
I drive through the night—*Vroom, vroom, vroom!*   (go fast)

I'm a little fire engine see my ladder,
Climb up to see what's the matter.   (move legs up and down)

I'm a little fire engine see my hose—*Squirt, squirt, squirt!*
Out the fire goes!   (hold hose)
Positive Parenting Praise! Good job acting like a fire engine.

Follow-Up Fun
Things That Go

Say & Sing

The Wheels on the Bus

The wheels on the bus
Go round and round,   (roll hands)
Round and round,
Round and round.
The wheels on the bus
Go round and round
All around the town.

What to Say

- Listen to a song about a bus.
- Let's sing the song and act it out together.

Positive Parenting Praise! Good job singing the song and acting it out.

- Let's sing the song again using other words, such as the people on the bus go—*Up and down;* the babies on the bus go—*Waa, waa, waa;* and the dogs on the bus go—*Woof, woof, woof!*

Follow-Up Fun
Things That Go

Draw & Write

Let's make a stop sign.

What You Need
drawing paper, crayons or markers, craft sticks, scissors, glue

What to Do

1. Draw a hexagon on the paper. As you point to each side, have children help you count—*1, 2, 3, 4, 5, 6.*

Positive Parenting Praise! Good job counting the sides of the hexagon.

2. Cut out the hexagon and write STOP on it. Name the letters as you write them. Ask children to name and trace the letters as they can.
3. Have children color their signs red.
4. Attach a craft stick to their stop signs.
5. Have children walk around stopping whenever they hold up their stop signs.

12

WEATHER

Before you read aloud one of the books listed below, preview the book and choose strategies modeled in the *Talkabouts* to support the development of early literacy concepts and skills.

It Is the Wind by Ferida Wolff, illustrated by James Ransome, Harper, 2005. A young child hears different sounds during the day, but it is the sound of the wind that puts him to sleep at night.

Little Mo, by Martin Waddell, illustrated by Jill Barton, Candlewick, 1993. A little polar bear learns to have fun sliding, gliding, twisting, and twirling on the ice on a cold day.

OH! by Kevin Henkes, Greenwillow, 1999. Children and animals play outside after a snowstorm.

Splash! by Flora McDonnell, Candlewick, 1999. Baby elephant shows elephant, tiger, and rhino how to cool off on a hot day.

Who Likes Rain? by Wong Herbert Yee, Holt, 2007. A young girl learns the answer to the title question after venturing outside during an April rain.

Follow-Up Fun
Weather

Act & Play

Let's pretend to go for a walk on a rainy day walk.

Let's put on our raincoats.
Put on our rain hats.
Put on our rain boots.
Positive Parenting Praise! Good job putting on your rain gear.

Let's go outside.
Open our umbrellas.
Walk in puddles—*Squish, squish, squish!*
Catch raindrops—*Splat, splat, splat!*
Oh, hear the thunder—*Boom, boom, boom!*

Let's run back to our houses.
Open the door.
Take off our rain boots.
Take off our rain hats.
Take off our raincoats.

Follow-Up Fun
Weather

Say & Sing

Eency, Weency Spider

Eency, weency spider   (raise hands)
Went up the waterspout.
Down came the rain   (lower hands)
And washed the spider out.
Out came the sun   (make a circle using hands)
And dried up all the rain.
So the eency, weency spider
Went up the spout again.   (raise hands)

What to Say

- Listen to a rhyme about a little spider and watch what I do with my hands.
- Say the rhyme with me using your hands to act it out.

Positive Parenting Praise! Good job reciting the rhyme and acting it out.

Follow-Up Fun
Weather

Draw & Write

Let's draw and write about a windy day.

What You Need
drawing paper, crayons or markers

What to Do

1. Ask children to draw a picture of a windy day.
2. Have children tell about their pictures.

Positive Parenting Praise! Good job telling about your windy day picture.

3. Encourage children to write their names on their pictures or trace the letters that you write.
4. Display their windy day pictures.

13

ABC'S

Before you read aloud one of the books listed below, preview the book and choose strategies modeled in the *Talkabouts* to support the development of early literacy concepts and skills.

ABC I Like Me! by Nancy Carlson, Viking, 1997. Letters of the alphabet suggest things that make children feel good about themselves.

Chicka Chicka Boom Boom by Bill Martin Jr and John Archambault, illustrated by Lois Ehlert, Simon & Schuster, 1989. Twenty-six alphabet letters find out that there is not enough room for all of them on top of a coconut tree.

The Everything Book by Denise Fleming, Holt, 2000. A variety of nursery rhymes, finger games, shapes, letters, numbers, colors, animals, and much more fill the colorful pages.

Max's ABC by Rosemary Wells, Viking, 2006. Max and Ruby introduce children to the alphabet with their humorous antics.

Mrs. McTats and Her Houseful of Cats by Alyssa Satin Capucilli, illustrated by Joan Rankin, Simon & Schuster, 2001. Mrs. McTats' cats and puppy have names that begin with different letters.

There is a list of more alphabet books on pages 141-142.

Follow-Up Fun
ABC's

Act & Play

Let's act out letters of the alphabet.

A, B, C—*C* is for *candle.*
Let's blow out a candle.

D, E, F—*F* is for *fish.*
Let's swim like fish.

G, H, I—*I* is for *ice cream.*
Let's eat an ice cream cone.

J, K, L—*L* is for *love.*
Let's give ourselves a hug.

M, N, O, P—*P* is for *paint.*
 Let's paint with a brush.
Positive Parenting Praise! Good job painting with a brush.

Q, R, S—*S* is for *sing.*
Let's sing a song.

T, U, V, W—*W* is for *worm.*
Let's wiggle like a worm.

X, Y, Z—*Z* is for *zipper.*
Let's zip up our jackets.

Follow-Up Fun
ABC's

The Alphabet Song

A-B-C-D-E-F-G,
H-I-J-K-L-M-N-O-P,
Q-R-S
T-U-V,
W-X-Y and Z

Now I know my ABC's.
Next time won't you sing with me?

What to Say

- Listen as I sing an alphabet song.
- Let's sing it together.

Positive Parenting Praise! Good job singing the song with me.

- Let's sing it again as we march around the room.

Follow-Up Fun
ABC's

Draw & Write

Let's make a letter tree.

What You Need
drawing paper, green construction paper, crayons or markers, scissors, glue

What to Do

1. Have children draw a tree on drawing paper.
2. Cut large leaves out of green construction paper.
3. Write children's names on the leaves or ask children to write them.
4. Have children glue the leaves on the trees.
5. Have available more large leaves. Encourage children to write letters or their names on the leaves and glue them on their trees.

Positive Parenting Praise! Good job writing letters on the leaves.

6. Display the trees so children can name the letters.

APPENDIX

MORE RECOMMENDED BOOKS TO READ ALOUD

Books for Infants and Toddlers

Baby Bear, Baby Bear, What Do You See? by Bill Martin Jr, illustrated by Eric Carle, Holt, 2007. Baby Bear sees animals that live in North America.

Baby Bear's Chairs by Jane Yolen, illustrated by Melissa Sweet, Gulliver, 2005. Mama, Papa, and Baby Bear have their own chairs, but Baby Bear's favorite is one that doesn't belong to him.

Bear Wants More by Karma Wilson, illustrated by Jane Chapman, Simon & Schuster, 2003. When Bear wakes up in the spring, his friends bring him food.

Big and Little by Margaret Miller, Greenwillow, 1998. Photographs reveal different sizes of familiar objects that fill a young child's world.

Big Wheels by Anne Rockwell, Walker, 1986. This book features vehicles with big wheels, such as bulldozers, dump trucks, and cranes.

The Bus for Us by Suzanne Bloom, Boyds Mills, 2001. Jess and a friend wait for the school bus that finally comes after a taxi, tow truck, fire engine, and other vehicles go by.

The Busy Little Squirrel by Nancy Tafuri, Simon & Schuster, 2007. Squirrel is too busy getting ready for winter to play with the other animals.

Busy Penguins by John Schindel and Jonathan Chester, Tricycle, 2000. A combination of colorful photographs and rhyming text help young children learn about penguins.

Carousel by Donald Crews, Greenwillow, 1982. Children enjoy a carousel ride as it comes alive through text and illustrations.

Chugga-Chugga Choo-Choo by Kevin Lewis, illustrated by Daniel Kirk, Hyperion, 1999. Rhyming text tells about a toy train that makes its way around the track in a boy's bedroom.

Close Your Eyes by Jean Marzollo, illustrated by Susan Jeffers, Dial, 1978. This rhyme is about a father who tries to put his young child to sleep.

Dig Dig Digging by Margaret Mayo, illustrated by Alex Ayliffe, Holt, 2002. Rhyming text and illustrations introduce vehicles, such as a bulldozer, tractor, crane, fire engine, and helicopter.

Dimity Duck by Jane Yolen, illustrated by Sebastien Braun, Philomel, 2006. After a day of playing with a friend, tired Dimity Duck returns home at night to go to bed.

Does a Kangaroo Have a Mother, Too? by Eric Carle, Harper, 2000. Children are introduced to baby animals and their mothers.

Firefighters! Speeding! Spraying! Saving! by Patricia Hubbell, illustrated by Viviana Garfoli, Cavendish, 2007. Firefighters hop on their trucks to put out fires.

From Head to Toe by Eric Carle, Harper, 1997. A young boy imitates different animal actions.

Good-Night, Owl! by Pat Hutchins, Simon & Schuster, 1972. Noisy animals keep Owl awake during the day while noisy Owl keeps them awake at night.

Goodnight Moon by Margaret Wise Brown, illustrated by Clement Hurd, Harper, 1947. In this classic book, a bunny says good night to familiar things in a bedroom.

Hello, Baby! by Mem Fox, illustrated by Steve Jenkins, Beach Lane, 2009. Rhyming text and bold illustrations introduce young children to a baby who meets a variety of animals.

Hello Toes! Hello Feet! by Ann Whitford Paul, illustrated by Nadine Bernard Westcott, DK, 1998. After greeting her feet when she wakes in the morning, a young girl continues to think about them during her busy day.

Inside Freight Train by Donald Crews, Harper, 2001. In this interactive book, children slide open the doors of each freight train car to see what is inside.

Jamberry by Bruce Degen, Harper, 1983. A boy and a bear go on a fun berry adventure through Berryland.

Llama, Llama, Red Pajama by Anna Dewdney, Viking, 2005. Baby Llama still wants Mama after listening to a bedtime story and being tucked into bed.

Oh My Baby Bear! by Audrey Wood, Harcourt, 1990. Baby Bear becomes Little Bear after he learns to do lots of things by himself.

Over in the Meadow by Paul Galdone, Aladdin, 1989. This adaptation of a classic counting rhyme introduces animals and their babies.

Peek-a-Moo! by Marie Torres Cimarusti, illustrated by Stephanie Petersen, Dutton, 1998. Repetitive text asks children to guess what animal is behind each flap in this interactive book.

Planes by Byron Barton, Harper, 1998. Similar in format to Barton's books *Trucks, Boats,* and *Trains,* one-line text describes how different airplanes are used.

Playground Day! by Jennifer Merz, Clarion, 2007. Children at the playground imitate what animals do.

Polar Bear, Polar Bear, What Do You Hear? by Bill Martin Jr, illustrated by Eric Carle, Holt, 1991. Polar Bear hears different zoo animal sounds.

Rabbits & Raindrops by Jim Arnosky, Putnam, 1997. Mother rabbit and her five baby rabbits play in the field in sun and rain.

Red Light, Green Light by Anastasia Suen, illustrated by Ken Wilson-Max, Harcourt, 2005. Colorful illustrations and simple rhyming text describe all kinds of things that go.

Red Rubber Boot Day by Mary Lyn Ray, illustrated by Lauren Stringer, Harcourt, 2000. A young boy keeps busy inside and out on a rainy day.

Rosie's Walk by Pat Hutchins, Simon & Schuster, 1968. This classic is about a fox that tries to catch a hen in a farmyard.

Snowballs by Lois Ehlert, Harcourt, 1995. Children learn about building a snow family using many objects.

Ten Apples Up on Top by Dr. Seuss, Random House, 1961. A dog, tiger, and lion balance apples on their heads until there is a crash in this humorous counting book.

Time to Say Goodnight by Sally Lloyd-Jones, illustrated by Jane Chapman, HarperCollins, 2006. At nighttime, animals go to sleep as does a young boy.

Today is Monday by Eric Carle, Philomel, 1993. Animals bring foods for others to eat on different days of the week.

Toot Toot Beep Beep by Emma Garcia, Boxer, 2008. In this noisy book, colorful cars share the road with a jeep, van, sports car, limousine, and taxi.

Tumble Bumble by Felicia Bond, Harper, 1996. The rhyming text in this story tells about a tiny bug that meets many animals as it goes on walk.

The Very Hungry Caterpillar by Eric Carle, Penguin, 1987. Numbers, days of the week, and names of foods are in this book about a caterpillar that builds a cocoon and becomes a butterfly.

What Does Bunny See? by Linda Sue Park, illustrated by Maggie Smith, Clarion, 2005. Bunny sees lots of colorful things during an adventure in a garden.

Where Is It? by Tana Hoban, Macmillan, 1974. Photographs show a rabbit looking for something special.

Where's Spot? by Eric Hill, Puffin, 1983. As mother looks for Spot in many different places, children lift the flaps in this interactive book to help find him.

Whoo! Whoo! Goes the Train by Anne Rockwell, Harper, 2009. Sound words help to tell the story of Alan's first train ride.

Whose Shoe? by Margaret Miller, Greenwillow, 1991. Words and photographs have children guessing about shoes.

Books for 3-to-5 Year Olds

All Aboard! by Mary Lyn Ray, illustrated by Amiko Hirao, Little, Brown, 2002. Funny pictures and text tell about a rabbit on an overnight train ride.

All for Pie, Pie for All by David Martin, illustrated by Valeri Gorbachev, Candlewick, 2006. The cat, mouse, and ant families all enjoy the apple pie baked by Grandma Cat.

Angelina Ballerina by Katharine Holabird, illustrated by Helen Craig, Pleasant, 2000. Angelina's dream of becoming a ballerina comes true after the little mouse takes dancing lessons.

Arthur's Nose by Marc Brown, Little Brown, 1976. After trying out different noses, Arthur decides he likes his nose best of all.

The Beastly Feast by Bruce Goldstone, illustrated by Blair Lent, Holt, 1998. Beasts bring yummy food to share at an animal feast.

Bunny Day by Rick Walton, illustrated by Paige Miglio, Harper, 2002. Bunny is busy with its family from breakfast to bedtime.

Busy, Busy Mouse by Virginia Kroll, illustrated by Fumi Kosaka, Viking, 2003. A family keeps busy morning until night and a mouse keeps busy from night until morning.

Caps for Sale by Esphyr Slobodkina, Harper, 1987. In this 1940's classic, monkeys busy themselves with monkey business while a peddler sleeps under a tree.

Cat Goes Fiddle-i-fee by Paul Galdone, Clarion, 1985. This traditional rhyme is about a boy and the farm animals that he feeds.

A Chair for My Mother by Vera B. Williams, Greenwillow, 1982. Rosa, along with her grandmother, and mother, save money to buy a new chair after a fire in their home destroys their belongings.

Chrysanthemum by Kevin Henkes, Greenwillow, 1991. Chrysanthemum wants to change her name after children make fun of it at school.

City Dog by Karla Kuskin, Clarion, 1994. City dog discovers the country during an exciting adventure to a new place.

Corduroy by Don Freeman, Viking, 1968. In this classic, a young girl visits a department store where she buys a bear with a missing button.

Curious George Rides a Bike by H. A. Rey, Houghton, 1993. George goes on an adventure as he rides his bike and eventually ends up in a circus.

EEK! There's a Mouse in the House by Wong Herbert Yee, Houghton, 1995. A young girl and animals try to catch a mouse running around in the house.

Harold and the Purple Crayon by Crockett Johnson, Harper, 1955. This classic story tells about an imaginary adventure that Harold's purple crayon takes him on.

Harry the Dirty Dog by Gene Zion, illustrated by Margaret Bloy Graham, Harper, 1956. In this classic, Harry runs away when he discovers that his family wants to give him a bath.

Here Comes the Night by Anne Rockwell, Holt, 2006. A young child goes through his bedtime routine with his mother.

If You Give a Mouse a Cookie by Laura Joffe Numeroff, illustrated by Felicia Bond, Harper, 1983. A bossy mouse is not satisfied with just a cookie, so it keeps a boy busy getting other things.

Inside Mouse, Outside Mouse by Lindsay Barrett George, Greenwillow, 2004. Two mice, one inside and one outside, keep themselves busy round the clock in their surroundings.

Kipper and Roly by Mick Inkpen, Harcourt, 2001. Kipper becomes attached to the birthday gift that he gives to Pig and ends up taking care of it.

Leo the Late Bloomer by Robert Kraus, illustrated by Jose Aruego, Windmill, 1971. Leo cannot do anything right, but eventually learns to do lots of things.

The Little Engine That Could by Watty Piper, illustrated by George Hauman and Doris Hauman, Grosset, 1978. Originally published in 1930, children learn an important lesson in this story about a little blue engine.

Little Green by Keith Baker, Harcourt, 2001. A young boy paints a picture of a hummingbird in a garden.

Lost! by David McPhail, Little, Brown, 1990. A little boy on his way to school makes friends with a lost bear.

Lucky Song by Vera B. Williams, Greenwillow, 1997. A young girl enjoys her family's attention throughout her day and lasting until bedtime.

Make Way for Ducklings by Robert McCloskey, Viking, 1941. This classic story is about Mr. and Mrs. Mallard's attempt to find a safe place for their eight baby ducklings.

Max Cleans Up by Rosemary Wells, Viking, 2000. Max cleans up his messy room with his sister Ruby's help.

May I Bring a Friend? by Beatrice Schenk de Regniers, illustrated by Beni Montresor, Atheneum, 1975. In this classic story, a boy brings his animal friends to visit in a castle.

Milton the Early Riser by Robert Kraus, illustrated by Jose Aruego and Ariane Dewey, Aladdin, 1987. Milton tries hard to wake up his animal friends in the early morning.

Mommies Say Shhh! by Patricia Polacco, Philomel, 2005. Animals make many sounds but mommies quiet them down.

Mouse Mess by Linnea Riley, Blue Sky, 1997. A little mouse makes a big mess while it looks for a snack in a kitchen at night.

Mr. Gumpy's Outing by John Burningham, Holt, 1970. Everyone wants to join Mr. Gumpy on his boat ride, but all are surprised when they fall in the river.

New Shoes, Red Shoes by Susan Rolling, Orchard, 2000. A young girl sees all kinds of shoes when she goes to buy new ones.

Noisy Nora by Rosemary Wells, Dial, 1977. Nora does many noisy and mischievous things to get her parents' attention while they take care of her siblings.

Olivia by Ian Falconer, Atheneum, 2000. A pig dressed all in red shows many things that she can do.

Our Class Took a Trip to the Zoo by Shirley Neitzel, illustrated by Nancy Winslow Parker, Greenwillow, 2002. The adventures of a class trip to the zoo are described in pictures and words.

Pass the Fritters, Critters by Cheryl Chapman, illustrated by Susan L. Roth, Harcourt, 1993. Animals gather around the table, but no food gets passed until the boy says the magic word.

Peter's Chair by Ezra Jack Keats, Viking, 1967. In this classic, Peter leaves home with his chair and dog after the arrival of a baby sister, but soon returns to his loving family.

Pigs Aplenty, Pigs Galore! by David McPhail, Dutton, 1993. A group of pigs finds it hard to leave after having a hilarious time in a house during the night.

The Rain Came Down by David Shannon, Blue Sky, 2000. Everyone gets grumpy when the rain comes down, but then they feel better when the rain stops.

Red Leaf, Yellow Leaf by Lois Ehlert, Harcourt, 1990. Lois Ehlert uses vibrant colors to show how a child plants a sugar maple tree.

The Runaway Bunny by Margaret Wise Brown, illustrated by Clement Hurd, Harper, 1991. In this 1942 classic, a bunny runs away several times, but is always retrieved by its loving mama.

Shape Capers by Cathryn Falwell, Greenwillow, 2007. Different shapes do many different things with young children.

Soggy Saturday by Phyllis Root, illustrated by Helen Craig, Candlewick, 2001. After turning blue from the rain, all the farm animals are painted so they look like themselves again.

Spring Is Here by Taro Gomi, Chronicle, 1989. Changes in the seasons are described in simple text.

There's an Alligator under My Bed by Mercer Mayer, Dial, 1987. A boy is determined to catch the alligator that is under his bed.

The Three Snow Bears by Jan Brett, Putnam, 2007. This version of the Goldilocks story is about an Inuit girl living in the Arctic.

Time To . . . by Bruce McMillan, Lothrop, 1989. Photographs and text describe each hour of a child's day from morning until night.

Titch and Daisy by Pat Hutchins, Greenwillow, 1996. Best friends Titch and Daisy have fun at a party only after discovering that they are both there.

Tracks in the Snow by Wong Herbert Yee, Holt, 2003. A little girl is curious about tracks that she sees in the snow.

Umbrella by Taro Yashima, Viking, 2004. Momo wants rain so she can use the boots and umbrella that she got for her birthday.

Way Down Deep in the Deep Blue Sea by Jan Peck, illustrated by Valeria Petrone, Simon & Schuster, 2004. A young child has a sea adventure while taking a bath.

Where the Wild Things Are by Maurice Sendak, Harper, 1988. This 1960's classic is filled with scary monsters that join Max in his wild adventure.

Zoom! Boom! Bully by Jon Scieszka, illustrated by David Shannon, Loren Long, and David Gordon, Simon & Schuster, 2008. Big

Rig is not a good friend to the other trucks because it knocks things down.

Alphabet Books

A You're Adorable words and music by Buddy Kaye, Fred Wise, and Sidney Lippman, illustrated by Martha Alexander, Candlewick, 1994. This popular alphabet song describes children's delightful traits.

ABC A Child's First Alphabet Book by Alison Jay, Dutton, 2003. Each page features a letter of the alphabet and an illustration of a familiar object to go along with it.

Action Alphabet by Shelley Rotner, Atheneum, 1996. Photographs show children engaged in activities such as running, swimming, and tugging.

Alfie's ABC by Shirley Hughes, Lothrop, 1997. This book tells about things Alfie likes to do with his family.

Alphabet Under Construction by Denise Fleming, Holt, 2002. A mouse works hard making the letters of the alphabet.

Annie, Bea, and Chi Chi Dolores by Donna Maurer, illustrated by Denys Cazet, Orchard, 1993. This alphabet book takes young children through a day in kindergarten.

Arf! Beg! Catch! by Henry Horenstein, Scholastic, 1999. A photograph of a dog is shown with a word for each letter.

The Bouncing, Dancing, Galloping ABC by Charlotte Doyle, illustrated by Julia Groton, Putnam, 2006. Two brothers move their way through this action alphabet book.

Dog's ABC by Emma Dodd, Dutton, 2000. This book describes the alphabet adventures of a dog as he wanders through his neighborhood throughout the day.

Flora McDonnell's ABC by Flora McDonnell, Candlewick, 1997. Letters of the alphabet are shown with colorful illustrations of animals and objects.

From Anne to Zach by Mary Jane Morton, illustrated by Michael Grejniec, Boyds Mill, 1996. Each letter is shown with a child's name to go with it.

G is for Goat by Patricia Polacco, Philomel, 2003. Goats on a farm are featured in this alphabet rhyming book.

The Guinea Pig ABC by Kate Duke, Dutton, 1983. Each page features a letter and single word to describe the antics of a lively guinea pig.

The Hullabaloo ABC by Beverly Cleary, illustrated by Ted Rand, Morrow, 1998. This alphabet book presents farm animals and activities in rhyme.

John Burningham's ABC by John Burningham, Jonathan Cape, 2000. Both uppercase and lowercase letters of the alphabet are shown with illustrations of objects.

K is for Kitten by Niki Clark Leopold, illustrated by Susan Jeffers, Putnam, 2002. A kitten is found and brought home to a loving family in this rhyming alphabet book.

Old Black Fly by Jim Aylesworth, illustrated by Stephen Gammell, Holt, 1992. This alphabet book tells about the adventures of an old black fly in rhyme.

So Many Bunnies by Rick Walton, illustrated by Paige Miglio, Lothrop, 1998. Rhyming text tells about a mother rabbit and her alphabet of 26 bunnies.

Rhyme, Fingerplay, and Song Books

Baby Beluga by Raffi, illustrated by Ashley Wolff, Crown, 1990

Down by the Bay by Raffi, Crown, 1988

Down by the Station by Will Hillenbrand, Gulliver, 1999

The Eeentsy Weentsy Spider Fingerplays and Action Rhymes by Joanne Cole and Stephanie Calmenson, illustrated by Alan Tiegreen, Morrow, 1991

Finger Rhymes collected and illustrated by Marc Brown, Dutton, 1980

Five Little Ducks illustrated by Ivan Bates, Orchard, 2006

Five Little Monkeys Jumping on the Bed by Eileen Christelow, Clarion, 1989

Going to the Zoo by Tom Paxton, illustrated by Karen Lee Schmidt, Morrow, 1996

Hand Rhymes collected and illustrated by Marc Brown, Dutton, 1985

Here We Go Round the Mulberry Bush by Willen Hillenbrand, Gulliver, 2003

The Hokey Pokey words by Larry La Prise, Charles P. Macak, Taftt Baker, illustrated by Sheila Hamanaka, Simon & Schuster, 1997

Hush Little Baby by Sylvia Long, Chronicle, 1997

Little White Duck lyrics by Walt Whippo, music by Bernard Zaritsky, illustrated by Joan Paley, Scholastic, 2001

Mary Engelbreit's Mother Goose by Mary Engelbreit, Harper, 2005

Miss Mary Mack adapted by Mary Ann Hoberman, illustrated by Nadine Bernard Westcott, Little, Brown, 2003

Mother Goose by Leo & Diane Dillon, Harcourt, 2008

Mother Goose by Sylvia Long, Chronicle, 1999

Mother Goose on the Loose by Hans Wilhelm, Sterling, 2009

My First Action Rhymes illustrated by Lynne Cravath, Harper, 2000

The Neighborhood Mother Goose by Nina Crews, Harper, 2004

Pat-a-Cake and other Play Rhymes by Joanne Cole and Stephanie Calmenson, illustrated by Alan Tiegreen, Morrow, 1992

Tomie dePaola's Mother Goose by Tomie dePaola, Putnam, 1985

OUR WORKSHOPS, BOOK, AND WEBSITE

OUR WORKSHOPS

We offer "Help Me Get Ready To Read" workshops for parents and grandparents, early childhood professionals, preschool staff, daycare providers, librarians, and volunteers in organizations that focus on early literacy. Also, we are available to present at regional and national professional conferences. In our interactive workshops, participants learn how to use read-aloud times effectively by

- **gaining** an understanding of early literacy concepts and skills;
- **acquiring** parenting strategies and reading strategies that enhance the read-aloud experience;
- **participating** in book-related activities that are specifically geared to develop early literacy concepts and skills; and
- **choosing** good books to read aloud based on suggested criteria.

OUR BOOK

Additional copies of *Help Me Get Ready To Read* can be purchased online. (www.readaloudguide.com or www.amazon.com) If you are interested in ordering large quantities of our book, contact us directly at our website. (www.readaloudguide.com) Discounts are available for bulk orders.

OUR WEBSITE

You may contact us at our website to get information about our workshops, order *Help Me Get Ready To Read*, or find out more about us. We look forward to hearing from you.
Website: www.readaloudguide.com

VOLUNTEER TO READ ALOUD IN YOUR COMMUNITY

Help Me Get Ready To Read Book Brigades

Take part in an exciting new service opportunity to help young children get ready to read. Organize a local *Help Me Get Ready To Read* Book Brigade by gathering volunteers to plan and run read-aloud times in your community.

Volunteers use *Help Me Get Ready To Read* as a training manual. It provides early literacy fundamentals and book-related activities to do during read-aloud sessions. The featured books in *Help Me Get Ready To Read* can be borrowed from public libraries, or purchased in bookstores or online.

Book Brigade members come from diverse groups, such as:

- high school students;
- college students;
- baby boomers including grandparents and retirees;
- religious and civic organizations;
- neighborhood book groups; and
- local businesses and corporations sponsoring community days.

Book Brigade volunteers contact local preschools, children's hospitals, pediatricians' offices, homeless shelters, daycare and early learning centers, and after-school programs to plan regularly scheduled read-aloud sessions. Book Brigade volunteers meet monthly to exchange ideas and share read-aloud experiences.

ABOUT US

Susan Marx, B.S.Ed, M.A. I am a parent educator, writer and editor of educational materials for students and teachers, and elementary classroom teacher. Over the past 17 years, I have led over 600 Families First positive parenting workshops for diverse groups of parents and professionals at homeless shelters, daycare centers, preschools, public and independent schools, worksites, and national early childhood conferences. Workshop topics include creating home-school partnerships, helping children succeed in school, understanding children's temperament, and getting children ready for kindergarten. I have appeared in parenting spots on Boston TV and cable networks, and have been interviewed by major newspapers and parenting magazines. As a writer and editor, I prepared materials for reading, social studies, spelling, and language arts textbooks and practice books for DC Heath, Silver Burdett Ginn, Macmillan, and Houghton Mifflin. In addition, I gave sales presentations to state textbook adoption committees. I also taught grades K through 5 in New York, California, and Massachusetts. I have three children and eight grandchildren.

Barbara Kasok, B.S.Ed. I am certified as a consulting teacher of reading in Massachusetts and have done graduate work in reading at Boston University and Lesley College. I taught in elementary school classrooms in Connecticut and Massachusetts, and in federally funded Title I reading programs (K-4) in Massachusetts. When I ran my own daycare program for children ages 1 to 3, reading aloud was an important part of each day. At Silver Burdett Ginn, a division of Simon and Schuster, I was a project manager responsible for working with teachers, freelance writers, and reading specialists from Boston University, University of Colorado, and University of Virginia to develop national reading programs for K-8. I recommended appropriate books for teaching reading in grades K-3, supervised editorial teams, interacted with book sales representatives, and delivered presentations on instructional delivery of reading content. I have also worked as a project manager to develop, write, and edit manuscript for K-8 reading, language arts, math, and social studies materials for national publishers, such as Houghton Mifflin, Harcourt, and Scholastic. These materials include reading lessons for teachers, reading practice books for children, decodable storybooks for beginning readers, and rhyme and poem books. I have three children and two grandchildren.

ACKNOWLEDGMENTS

Thanks to our husbands, Michael and Ed, for their support while we were busy writing this guide—from operating computers to baking cookies, and from handling finances to reading manuscript. Having them beside us for the past 43 years has made our journeys—whether raising our children or writing this book—a blessing for sure.

Our thanks to a talented group of supporters and reviewers who contributed to our book by sharing their ideas based on their professional and personal experiences as classroom teachers, elementary school principals, editors, parents, and grandparents—Betty Cummings Clark, Mary Carreiro, Helen Guzzi, Debbie O'Brien, Carol Salvi, and Carol Sanzone. Our special thanks go to Sharon Kasok, Sarah Kasok, Susan MacLeod, and Amy Marx for taking time during their busy lives to give us feedback and encouragement.

Above all, thanks to our children, grandchildren, and the many children in our classrooms over the years, for sharing precious read-aloud moments with us.

SUGGESTED READINGS ABOUT EARLY LITERACY

Adams, M.J. (1990). *Beginning to read: Thinking and learning about print.* Cambridge, MA: MIT Press.

Allington, R., & Cunningham, P. (2002). *Classrooms that Work. They Can All Read and Write.* New York: Allyn & Bacon.

Anderson, R.C., Hiebert, E.H., Scott, J.A., & Wilkinson, I.A.G. (1985). *Becoming a Nation of Readers: The Report of the Commission on Reading.* Champaign, IL: Center for the Study of Reading; Washington, DC: National Institute of Education.

Apel, K., & Masterson, J. (2001). *Beyond Baby Talk: From Sounds to Sentences, a Parent's Guide to Language Development.* Roseville, CA: Prima Publishing.

Armbruster, B., Lehr, Fran, and Osborn, Jean. (2003). *A Child Becomes a Reader Birth through Preschool.* Washington, DC: National Institute for Literacy.

Burns, M.S., Griffin, P., & Snow, C.E. (Eds.). (1999). *Starting Out Right: A Guide to Promoting Children's Reading Success.* Washington, D.C.: National Academy Press.

Clay, Marie. (2000). *Concepts About Print: What Have Children Learned About the Way We Print Language?* Portsmouth, NH: Heinemann.

Clay, Marie. (1983). *The early detection of reading difficulties,* third edition. Portsmouth, NH: Heinemann.

Developing Early Literacy: Report of the National Early Literacy Panel. (2008). Washington, DC: National Institute for Literacy.

McGee, Lea, M. and Richgels, Donald, J. (2008). *Literacy's Beginnings: Supporting Young Readers and Writers,* fifth edition. New York: Allyn & Bacon.

Neuman, S., Copple, C., Bredekamp, S. (2000). *Learning to Read and Write: Developmentally Appropriate Practices for Young Children.* Washington D.C.: National Association for the Education of Young Children.

Snow, C. E., Burns, M. S., & Griffin, P. (Eds.). (1998). *Preventing reading difficulties in young children.* Washington, DC: National Academy Press.

Strickland, Dorothy, S. & Morrow, Lesley Mandel. (2000) *Beginning Reading and Writing.* New York: Teachers College Press.

Strickland, Dorothy, S. & Morrow, Lesley Mandel. (Eds.). (1989) *Emerging Literacy: Young Children Learn to Read and Write.* Newark, DE: International Reading Association.

INDEX OF BOOK TITLES

Here is a complete list of recommended books to read aloud in *Help Me Get Ready To Read*. See indicated pages for more information about each book.

Bee-bim Bop! by Linda Sue Park, 105
Beep, Beep, Let's Go! by Eleanor Taylor, 83
Big and Little by Margaret Miller, 131
Big Fat Hen by Keith Baker, 11
Big Red Barn by Margaret Wise Brown, 43
Big Wheels by Anne Rockwell, 131
Black on White by Tana Hoban, 11
Blue Goose by Nancy Tafuri, 14
Blue Hat, Green Hat by Sandra Boynton, 11
The Bouncing, Dancing, Galloping ABC by Charlotte Doyle, 141
Bread Bread Bread by Ann Morris, 73
The Bridge is Up! by Babs Bell, 11
Brown Bear, Brown Bear, What Do You See? by Bill Martin Jr, 109
Bumpety Bump! by Pat Hutchins, 14
Bunny Bungalow by Cynthia Rylant, 15
Bunny Day by Rick Walton, 136
The Bus for Us by Suzanne Bloom, 131
Busy, Busy Mouse by Virginia Kroll, 136
The Busy Little Squirrel by Nancy Tafuri, 132
Busy Penguins by John Schindel and Jonathan Chester, 132
Caps for Sale by Esphyr Slobodkina, 136
Carousel by Donald Crews, 132
The Carrot Seed by Ruth Krauss, 105
Cat Goes Fiddle-i-fee by Paul Galdone, 136
A Chair for My Mother by Vera B. Williams, 136
Chicka Chicka Boom Boom by Bill Martin Jr and John Archambault, 125
Chicken Bedtime Is Really Early by Erica S. Perl, 15
Chicken Little by Rebecca Emberley and Ed Emberley, 109
Chrysanthemum by Kevin Henkes, 136
Chugga-Chugga Choo-Choo by Kevin Lewis, 132
City Dog by Karla Kuskin, 136
City Dog, Country Frog by Mo Willems, 101
Clap Your Hands by Lorinda Bryan Caulcy, 11
Close Your Eyes by Jean Marzollo, 132
Corduroy by Don Freeman, 137
The Cow Loves Cookies by Karma Wilson, 109
Curious George Rides a Bike by H. A. Rey, 137
Dancing Feet by Lindsey Craig, 11
The Deep Blue Sea by Audrey Wood, 53

Made in the USA
Lexington, KY
19 December 2010